AF269712

COMMUNICATION MYTHS

COMMUNICATION MYTHS

What We Know That Isn't So and What We Need to Know

J. Dan Rothwell

BLOOMSBURY ACADEMIC
NEW YORK · LONDON · OXFORD · NEW DELHI · SYDNEY

BLOOMSBURY ACADEMIC
Bloomsbury Publishing Inc, 1385 Broadway, New York, NY 10018, USA
Bloomsbury Publishing Plc, 50 Bedford Square, London, WC1B 3DP, UK
Bloomsbury Publishing Ireland, 29 Earlsfort Terrace, Dublin 2,
D02 AY28, Ireland

BLOOMSBURY, BLOOMSBURY ACADEMIC and the Diana logo are
trademarks of Bloomsbury Publishing Plc

First published in the United States of America 2025

Cover design: Dustin Watson

Bloomsbury Publishing Inc does not have any control over, or responsibility for, any third-party websites referred to or in this book. All internet
addresses given in this book were correct at the time of going to press. The
author and publisher regret any inconvenience caused if addresses have
changed or sites have ceased to exist, but can accept no responsibility for any
such changes.

Library of Congress Cataloging-in-Publication Data Available

ISBN: HB: 979-8-8818-0626-2
      ePDF: 979-8-8818-6697-6
      eBook: 979-8-8818-0627-9

Typeset by Deanta Global Publishing Services, Chennai, India
Printed and bound in the United States of America

For product safety related questions contact productsafety@bloomsbury.com.

To find out more about our authors and books visit www.bloomsbury.com
and sign up for our newsletters.

To my immensely talented, compassionate, and loving wife, Marcy.
No better partner in life could be imagined.

CONTENTS

PART IV   PUBLIC SPEAKING

PREFACE

I was a painfully shy boy who preferred to meld into the shadows of my elementary school environment, so my choice to make communication my professional life's work may seem surprising. I credit my parents who, ignoring my protestations, insisted that I join the high school debate team to bring me out of my social phobic shell (see Chapter 18). Unexpectedly, I found a niche for gradually building my confidence and self-esteem, and to my great surprise, public speaking became a continually exhilarating experience. Beyond debate and public speaking, I grew to appreciate that the knowledge and application of a broad range of communication competencies, discussed in each chapter of this book, can be invaluable in navigating personal and professional relationships. Every person, no matter their temperament and personality, can benefit from a greater understanding of human communication in a myriad of contexts.

Unfortunately, common myths about communication, the misconceptions and misinformation about this most critical human activity, swamp the Internet and social media. They clutter our minds with nonsense and dangerous mental refuse that can destroy relationships, place us in harm's way, and contribute to the political and personal polarization that infects our public and private discourse.

They prevent us from relating to one another in the most effective and beneficial ways.

In this book, I expose almost two dozen of these most prevalent communication myths. Here are some examples: Competent communication is just common sense, so say the uninformed. Almost all communication is nonverbal, we are persistently told in popular publications. Venting your anger reduces it, counsel self-designated experts on the Internet. Certain traits make a person an effective leader, we hear from the charisma consultants. Ignore the experts on controversial issues we debate, and study instead at the University of Google, shout the uninformed in their ALL-CAPS online messages. It is past time to jettison these and other myths that spread across our rhetorical landscape before we toboggan uncontrollably down the slippery slope of abject ignorance that leads to tumult and, without rational guardrails, potential disaster.

My fondest hope when I played Little League and Pony League baseball was that I would eventually become a Hall of Fame major league baseball pitcher. Don't bother consulting Google. It didn't happen. Instead, my subsequent hope once my inflated dream of athletic stardom went unrealized became making a small contribution to the betterment of our collective discourse by teaching at five colleges and writing seven books on communication. If *Communication Myths* contributes to your growth as a competent communicator, then that will be my solace for a failed athletic career.

ACKNOWLEDGMENTS

In the process of writing seven books published in 24 editions spanning several decades, I have worked with many capable editors, assistant editors, and teams of behind-the-scenes professionals who have helped me have a successful career as an author. You know who you are! Please accept my heartfelt thanks. I am not providing a list of your names for two reasons. First, the list would be gigantic and not fascinating reading. Second, I do not wish to emulate the Oscar and Emmy award programs in which winners mount the stage and list names of individuals completely unfamiliar to almost everyone in the massive television audience.

Nevertheless, I do want to single out two individuals who have been instrumental in bringing *Communication Myths* to fruition. Jaime Burns, portfolio manager for communication at Oxford University Press, who shepherded three of my books to completion, steadfastly resisted my vigorous attempts to have OUP publish *CM*. Instead, she suggested that I pursue a contract from Rowman & Littlefield (now Bloomsbury Academic) as a more appropriate landing spot. She was right. Once I got linked to executive editor Natalie Mandziuk at

Bloomsbury Academic, my foray into the vast world of trade books instead of textbooks emerged. Both individuals have been a joy to work with despite our occasional disagreements. You are true professionals in every positive sense of that word. You have my sincerest appreciation.

Part I

COMMUNICATION BEDROCK

1

MYTH: COMMUNICATION IS SIMPLY EXCHANGING INFORMATION

American humorist Will Rogers reputedly remarked, "It isn't what we don't know that gives us trouble; it's what we know that ain't so." Foolish behavior can arise from holding rigidly to *myths*—beliefs or ideas contradicted or shown to be misrepresented by fact and reasoning. Communication myths, the central focus of this book, are the termites of human relationships, undermining our most important means of connecting with other people. What I present in almost two dozen chapters are the most consequential communication myths that can adversely affect our relationships and ultimately our success in life in a wide variety of arenas—at home, at work, in groups, and at public venues. As you will see, building relationships with a mythical foundation can easily collapse them into dust.

Additionally, *I will provide a recurring explanation and application of what constitutes communication competence, the antidote for the virus-like spread of communication myths*. Human communication is key to our identity as a species, our self-concept, our psychological and physical well-being, and our very existence. Separating myth from fact on this essential daily activity deserves not only extensive scrutiny but also concentration on how to vastly improve our communication with the panoply of people that inhabit our planet.

Let's begin with the most basic communication myth—namely, defining the essence of human communication as the mere "act of exchanging information." This is a common myth, especially prevalent on numerous Internet sites.[1] It is an inaccurately narrow and superficial definition of human communication. It is tantamount to defining mathematics as "manipulating numbers" or English as "a study of words."

Defining human communication as "exchanging information" misrepresents its nature and undermines its frequent life-altering importance. For example, consider a person unexpectedly dumping their longtime intimate partner by text messaging them: "I fell in love with someone else. I didn't expect this to happen but it did. I'll be moving out. It is what it is." So now should we anticipate the ex-partner's response to be just a dispassionate exchange of information, such as, "OK, message received." Really? You aren't exchanging dessert recipes. A person's life is likely thrown into emotional upheaval.

The significance of *emotional intelligence*—"managing feelings so that they are expressed appropriately and effectively"[2]—is not apparent or even vaguely included in the "exchanging information" definition. The hypothetical breakup example highlights this. The instigator of the breakup offers an indifferent text message notification as a mere information exchange. There isn't even a lame attempt to show empathy, a key aspect of emotional intelligence. *Empathy* shows genuine concern for the other person, views the situation from their perspective without judgment, and relates to their feelings of sadness, anger, or other emotions. The terse message from the breakup initiator doesn't express a scintilla of concern for any emotional damage done to the jilted partner. Even the choice to announce the demise of the relationship via text message as a mere information exchange can seem cowardly by purposely avoiding an uncomfortable, potentially volatile face-to-face confrontation. If you think that this impersonal means of breaking up with an intimate partner is just hypothetical and highly unusual, think again. Survey results reveal that it is strikingly common in our media-obsessed landscape.[3]

The imaginative predictions both effusive and scary for ChatGPT further underline the mythical view of human communication as just a robot-like exchange of information. This admittedly fascinating emerging technology has and will continue to advance "human-like responses to natural language queries and prompts," notes Dr. Rodrigue Rizk, an expert on ChatGPT. He further notes, however, that it is technology essentially for "exchanging information" between humans and computers.[4] ChatGPT may be "humanlike," but it isn't actually human communication any more than Siri is a member of anyone's circle of friends. For all its potential benefits, ChatGPT cannot substitute for the immeasurable value of human connection (see especially Chapter 10). You won't experience the social bonding that results from having a beer and a lengthy chat with a close friend at your local tavern by substituting an exchange of information with nonhuman ChatGPT. Our brains "are wired to be social. . . . We are naturally curious about what is going on in the minds of other people"[5] There is no ChatGPT mind about which to be curious. That is why it is called *artificial* intelligence.

So, since defining human communication as an exchange of information widely misses the mark, how should it be defined? I begin by building the definition from an examination of its individual parts. The root of the word *communication* is from the Latin word *communicare*, which means "to share" or make common. You aren't merely passing information back and forth in pickleball fashion when you communicate. You try to share meaning with other people. *Meaning* is "the conscious pattern humans create out of their interpretation of experience"[6] It is derived from making sense of messages communicated. When individuals communicate with each other, they reconstruct messages received both cognitively and emotionally, attempting to understand them as intended by senders. This is no small task.

Two people only approximate the meaning communicated for an idea, concept, relationship, experience, or even a symbol. Overlapping interpretations, not exact meaning, are the best that you can expect. For example, coworkers may perceive each other as friends. The meaning of that friendship, however, and the depth of such a relationship is not identical. There are always at the very least subtle differences and sometimes embarrassing ones, such as when one person perceives the friendship as strictly social but the other person sees it as possibly romantic. Awkward!

Sharing meaning with others recognizes communication as a dynamic process, ever changing, and continuous. You can't comprehend the essence of human communication by focusing statically only on single words, sentences, or gestures that package information, any more than you can determine the essence of the ocean by taking a picture of a wave or scooping up a glass of salt water. You can meaningfully study the ocean only in its complexity—the waves, tides and currents, flora and fauna, and so forth. Similarly, to comprehend the essence of human communication, you must study currents of thoughts and emotions expressed every day both verbally and nonverbally in the context of dynamic, persistent change.

This dynamic process of sharing meaning with others involves numerous elements. When you initiate communication with other people, you are the *sender* who *encodes* your ideas, or *message*, by organizing and expressing them over a *channel*, or medium such as by phone, text, or in person, to *receivers*, who *decode*, or interpret verbal and nonverbal messages from others, who provide *feedback*, or verbal and nonverbal responses. Add to this *fields of experience*, which are your frames of reference that include your accumulated life experiences, ethnicity, cultural background, gender identity, and geographic background, and *noise*, which is any interference with effective transmission and reception of your message. Also, human communication occurs within a *context*, which is composed of who communicates what, to whom, and why they do it; where it happens; when it takes place; and how it is accomplished.

Considering these elements of the communication process, there is a final part of the human communication definition to address—namely, that communication is *transactional*. This means that speakers and listeners are both *senders and receivers simultaneously*, not exclusively one or the other. When acting primarily as a sender, you are receiving listeners' feedback, and when engaged primarily as a receiver, you are also providing feedback to senders at the same time. *This feedback impacts all parties within its context.* When group members are glued to their smartphones during a meeting and not listening to your presentation, plodding on without attempting to rejuvenate your listeners' attention means you are talking to yourself. You might as well distribute a handout and sit down. You need to adjust to the feedback, recognizing that listeners' attention requires rejuvenation by employing attention strategies (see Chapter 19). Listeners also need to focus on the speaker because, as anyone who has given a presentation to a lethargic group knows, inattentive listeners can drain a speaker's motivation and enthusiasm.

So, now that I have identified its many elements, I can provide a definition of *human communication* in its essence as *a dynamic transactional process of sharing meaning with other people*. But wait, there are still remaining complexities related to what I have discussed so far that require elaboration and complete the case that defining human communication as a mere exchange of information is a myth.

First, there are two dimensions inherent in any message.[7] The *content dimension* refers to the exchange of information. The *relationship dimension* refers to how a message defines or redefines the connection between individuals, a part that is missing from the exchanging information definition. "Please pick up packages from our department mail slot; thank you" and "Pick up packages from our department mail slot" both have the same basic content or transfer of information about collecting packages, but the first message shows respect and politeness; the second message is a command with an overtone of power inequity.

Second, channel choice is clearly consequential. Information isn't just tossed back and forth without consideration of the effectiveness of the channel chosen for sharing meaning. For example, much has been made of the effects of the use of social media and smartphone texting. People seem slightly startled to receive actual phone calls anymore. It's as though we wonder whether, instead of rapidly thumb typing text messages, crippling carpal thumb-al syndrome has suddenly struck friends, coworkers, and others, reluctantly necessitating phone conversation. With some agreed-upon exceptions with friends and family members, the recent rule of thumb for cellphone etiquette is to text first and ask for permission to call. Unexpected cellphone calls are considered intrusive.[8] We talk less and text more, substituting emojis for more direct nonverbal communication, but a phone conversation is a far superior channel for in-depth discussions and creating social bonds between people than is text messaging.[9] Hearing a person's voice matters because it "conveys a myriad of emotions" mostly absent from texting.[10] Texting, of course, certainly has its advantages, not the least of which is never feeling trapped by a loquacious friend who ignores your signoff, "Well, I should be going," and obliviously keeps talking while you struggle to find a polite but effective way of ending the marathon conversation.

Careless use of electronic communication channels can produce some embarrassing message clunkers. Note one individual's Tweet (X-post?).[11] Commenting on an athlete's legendary status, one message poster clearly meant to say "immortal" but left out the "t' and said "immoral" instead. My wife texted a colleague at work about a delicious "nut taco" recipe. Autocorrect, unhelpfully, altered it to "butt taco"—not so delicious.

Third, your fields of experience are your constant companions, traveling with you to every communication event, impacting your communication with others. As a notable aside, LLMs (large language models) such as ChatGPT "have never experienced anything. They are just programs that have ingested unimaginable amounts of text," notes Michael Wooldridge, professor of computer science at Oxford University. He continues, "LLMs might do a great job at describing the sensation of being drunk, but this is only because they have read a lot of descriptions of being drunk. They have not, and cannot, experience it themselves. They have no purpose other than to produce the best response to the prompt you give them."[12] Your fields of experience are unique to you. ChatGPT can't truly replicate them, and neither can any other person.

When fields of experience are poorly matched between individuals, they can precipitate misunderstanding, even discrimination and hatred. Ascertaining commonalities in mutual fields of experience—in other words, analyzing your audience—can cultivate empathy and compassion. Every transaction, good or bad, with another person is a foothold on your next communication transaction, and your accumulated experiences influence each new conversation and communication event.

Consider this one dramatic experience. A very close friend of mine named Terry, a colleague who taught psychology at my college, was inexplicably violently attacked by a mentally ill former student at the end of a class. Terry was struck in the face with an axe handle. Three male students immediately jumped the attacker and restrained him until campus police arrived. Meanwhile, Terry bled profusely from his severe facial injury that later required reconstructive plastic surgery. Just imagine Terry returning to the classroom upon his recovery. Clearly, this experience had a deep and lasting effect on his feelings of security and whether he ever felt totally comfortable returning to work. Aside from Terry's experience, the entire campus was thunderstruck by this seemingly random act of violence. These experiences become part of our bank account of accumulated memories affecting our ensuing communication with others.

Fourth, change any aspect of the context and the results can be enormously different. For example, saying disparaging remarks about your boss in guarded conversations to gain favor with like-minded coworkers is far different than saying the very same things to your boss's face. When American dignitaries and businesspeople travel to Japan, one source of awkward social interaction is the bowing ritual used as a social greeting. Americans are not accustomed to bowing, and when they are required to do so in order not to offend, they often perform it with the gracefulness of 300-pound NFL linemen ballet dancing. Failure to follow the Japanese rules associated with the bowing ritual in cross-cultural interactions can produce perceptions of disrespect. Bowing in the United States, however, is likely to be perceived as communicating subservience. Picture that students at an American college are told to bow each time a particular status-conscious professor enters the classroom. Now imagine students dropping the class.

Lastly, the concept of noise in a communication transaction is diverse and complicated. There are four kinds. The most obvious is *physical noise*, or external environmental distractions, such as a disruptive cellphone ringtone, poorly heated rooms, coworkers arriving late to a meeting and interrupting the proceedings as they nudge their way to the nearest seat in a crowded room, or an applicant for a professional job appearing before an interviewing panel dressed in plaid shorts and a T-shirt with the statement "Fake It Till You Make It" (a real example).

There is *physiological noise*, or biological influences, such as anxiety while waiting to be interviewed for an important job. Feeling ill, lethargic, or burned out from overwork are additional examples. A Future Forum global survey of 10,243 desk-based workers polled in six countries found that 42% reported burnout from physical exhaustion.[13] "By working faithfully 8 hours a day, you may eventually get to be the boss and work 12 hours a day," said poet Robert Frost prosaically. Burnout can cause additional physiological noise such as sleeplessness and depression.

Psychological noise is the preconceptions, biases, and assumptions that impede effective message transmission and reception. DEI (diversity, equity, inclusion) efforts have the support of a majority of workers surveyed by Pew Research,[14] but political backlash against such programs in organizations and institutions has arisen. The psychological noise from controversy associated with DEI efforts has sometimes become highly distracting from their noble intent.

Finally, there is *semantic noise* produced by word choice. A prime example is the ever-changing debate on what is the acceptable or preferred term for various ethnic groups. Should you choose the term *African American* or *Black*? Is *Native American* or *American Indian* the preferred term? Pew Research found that, among relevant ethnic respondents surveyed, 52% preferred the designation *Hispanic*, 29% preferred *Latino*, and a scant 4% preferred *Latinx*, a gender-neutral term increasingly popular among various media.[15] To complicate this further, *Latine* has increasing acceptance, especially among 18- to 29-year-olds, as a substitute for *Latinx*.[16] Different individuals and groups have term preferences. Choosing the "wrong" term can derail your message by drawing attention to terminological disagreements.

Recently, gender terminology has entered the semantic noise arena with the increasing but controversial use of the gender-neutral singular "they" instead of the binary "he" or "she." For example, "The person who sent us congratulations on our victory was thoughtful. *They* should be commended." Some people object, arguing that "they" cannot "logically" be a singular pronoun. The objection to the singular "they," however, ignores history. For centuries, authors such as Chaucer, Jane Austen, Lord Byron, and others often used "they" as a singular pronoun until the 18th century, when such usage was discouraged in schools. Nevertheless, "they" remained in common usage in its gender neutrality outside of academic settings.[17] Even within academia, "they" as a singular, gender-neutral pronoun has been accepted by the American Dialect Society[18] and by the American Psychological Association for its style manual.[19]

In summary, defining communication as a mere exchange of information clearly is a myth because it is simplistic and misconstrues the true nature of this critical activity. Human communication is a dynamic transactional process of sharing meaning with other people. Despite the numerous elements of this definition already discussed, what I have presented so far is no more than an initial sketch of the enormously complex process. As I unfold many additional communication myths and explore communication competence as the antidote in ensuing chapters, this exploration will sweep out some of the musty misconceptions many people have stored in their mental attics regarding human communication.

②

MYTH: COMMUNICATION IS JUST COMMON SENSE

All of us have communicated our entire lives. Is there any behavior we do more often than communicate? Unless a person is an out-of-touch survivalist hiding as a recluse in a cave, it is the most integral activity that pervades our daily human experience. Even if you ghost someone you are still communicating, although the message can be confusing ("Have I offended them?"; "Did they not receive my texts?").

Given our abundant communication experience and its pervasiveness, it is easy to vastly overestimate what we think we know that isn't so about communicating competently with other people. Experience isn't always the best teacher, especially if that experience is mostly based on myths. To convince my college students that common sense is a slippery, unreliable guidepost for knowing how to communicate competently, I regularly tested them on their general knowledge of communication. Correct or incorrect answers were determined based on abundant research. Students took this test during the very first class period of the semester. There were no technical definitions of concepts or questions about theories or obscure facts. All questions were well within the average college student's communication experience. If communication is just common sense and experience is a reliable teacher, then acing this quiz should have been an elementary undertaking. Almost all students, however, flunked the exam every semester without variation, and of the thousands of students who completed the quiz over the many years that I conducted this activity, no one received an A grade, and only a handful reached even a low B. (No, the grade didn't count. I didn't want a riot on the first day of class.) I was never surprised by these poor results, and they were never reason for ridicule. The reasons for taking a communication course or reading this book should be to learn new information, to acquire new insights, and to dispel the communication myths popular culture often spreads in casual abundance. What we think we know about communication so often just isn't so.

Taking a broader view, cultural differences dramatically contradict the myth that communication competence is just common sense. *Value differences* are variations in the significance placed on deeply held views of what is right, good, and worthwhile. Value differences highlight vast distinctions between individualist and collectivist cultures, but they must be learned, not grasped from common sense. *Individualist cultures* typically value personal autonomy and competitiveness, privacy, individual liberties, and toleration of nonconformity even if it is sometimes disruptive. *Collectivist cultures* typically value intragroup cooperation and conformity and personal sacrifice for the sake of group harmony.[1] North American–, Western European–, and European-influenced cultures such as Australia and New Zealand fall into the individualist category. East Asian, North African, and most Latin American cultures fall into the collectivist category. About 70% of the global population resides in collectivist cultures.[2]

One survey asked a broad range of respondents in eight East Asian countries and the United States, "Which of the following are critically important to your people?"[3] The comparisons starkly underline the deep value differences between individualist and collectivist cultures.

	Asians	Americans
1. Individual rights	29%	73%
2. Personal freedom	32%	82%
3. An orderly society	70%	11%

No culture is completely individualist or collectivist. Some individuals may disagree with the prevailing values of their culture. Nevertheless, there are strong cultural value tendencies one way or the other. Entering a culture whose values are distinctly different from yours without studying widely accepted behavioral rules and expectations can make you wish that you hadn't fallen victim to the "just common sense" communication myth likely to result in avoidable blunders. For example, a student in my class shared an experience she had while hitchhiking in Greece. She repeatedly tried to "thumb a ride" in the usual way Americans do by sticking out her upraised thumb as drivers passed. For more than two hours, she was not only unsuccessful in hitching a ride, but she was admittedly flustered by the frequent hand gestures and yelling that indicated nasty insults from drivers and passengers. What she didn't realize until later is that the thumbs-up gesture in Greece is an obscenity, tantamount to "up yours," to put it delicately.[4]

These cultural value differences are starkly reflected in communication styles that defy an intuitive understanding. A low-context communication style is characteristic of individualist cultures. A high-context communication style is characteristic of a collectivist culture.[5] The chief distinction is in verbal expression. A *low-context communication style* is verbally explicit, assertive, and self-enhancing. Free expression of opinions and public speaking ability are highly valued. "Say what you mean and mean what you say" and "Be direct not ambiguous" are statements that reflect a low-context communication style. By contrast, a *high-context communication style* is characterized by indirect verbal expression. "Reading between the lines" by recognizing rules and unspoken expectations is assumed. For example, a response such as "I'll think about it" should usually be interpreted as a face-saving way of saying no in Japan.[6] From the Japanese perspective, failure to understand what should be obvious from the cultural context can make an American seem a bit dense. From an American perspective, however, it may seem that one must be a mind reader to accurately grasp the meaning of what seems like a straightforward message that should be taken literally.[7] Common sense won't discern such differences in perspective and expectations.

If communication competence consists mostly of common sense, with no requirement for studying or training even when cultural values dramatically differ, then why does research show that people often communicate with the grace and effectiveness of an inebriated celebrity at an awards ceremony?[8] Extensive research reveals that poor communication is central to interpersonal relationship failure.[9] Many studies report that college students vastly overrate their oral communication skills when compared to employers' assessments of them.[10] Similarly, almost all self-identified leaders of corporate virtual teams rate themselves as "effective" or "very effective," but fewer than one-fifth of team members agree.[11] Research conducted by Grammarly Business and the Harris organization concluded that "poor workplace communication is a pervasive problem burdening businesses and employees alike." The study estimates a $1.2 trillion annual loss among U.S. businesses caused by poor communication.[12] Several studies of the health care industry document that poor communication frequently leads to serious medical errors, patient deaths, and medical malpractice suits.[13]

Ironically, the greater the communication incompetence, the greater is the inflated self-assessments of communication ability. This exaggerated sense of self-accomplishment and self-worth is called the *Dunning-Kruger effect*—incompetence stymies self-awareness of one's limitations.[14] Common sense is of little help when individuals have limited self-awareness of their communication deficiencies. Without education and training, that is not likely to improve. For example, in a CareerBuilder survey of 1,014 hiring managers and human resources professionals among businesses of varying sizes, respondents' reports of candidates' gaffes included: candidate asked for a cocktail during the interview; candidate wore a Darth Vader outfit; and candidate offered pumpkins to the interviewer because they "transfer good energy."[15] Another survey by CareerBuilder of more than 3,000 professionals nationwide included these reported jaw-dropping blunders: candidate answered cellphone and asked the interviewer to leave her own office because it was a "private" call; candidate told the interviewer he was fired for beating up his last boss; and candidate said she couldn't provide a writing sample because all of her writing was for the CIA and was classified.[16] None of these candidates were hired, but all of them with an apparent insufficient awareness of their communication deficiencies applied for professional jobs and were likely surprised by their rejection.

Note that what passes in the popular media and culture for knowledge and insight about communicating competently, and what may seem like common sense, is often pure myth. How do I know? Because voluminous research says so! Communicating competently is not a simple, commonsense process. Consider briefly its consequential complexity.

Communication competence is engaging in communication with other people that is perceived to be both appropriate and effective in a specific context.[17] *Appropriateness* means that you strive to tailor your messages to the expectations of your receivers. This requires understanding the rules embedded in every communication context whether the rules are apparent or unobtrusive. A *rule* "is a prescription that indicates what behavior is obligated, prohibited, or preferred in a given context."[18] Some rules are *explicit* (directly expressed), such as stated prohibitions about cellphone usage during meetings and smoking in restaurants. Then there is this sign that I came across in Australia: "NO PARKING: Vehicles will be shredded and turned into beer cans." Now that's explicit!

Most rules, however, are *implied* or indicated indirectly by patterns of behavior. Common sense has little to do with dictating many implicit rules. For example, some households prefer removing one's shoes before entering the home. The rule can be implicitly ascertained by seeing the mountain of footwear at the entrance. When asked by a coworker or friend, even a stranger, "How ya doing?" the typical implicit rule deduced from observing others is to respond, "I'm fine, how are you?"—even if your dog died, your computer was stolen, and your spouse left you. Cultural greeting rules dictate that the question shouldn't be interpreted literally. Consequently, the greeting becomes ritualistic, even mindless, which is why you may have caught yourself on more than one occasion, as I have done, asking, "How are you?" and receiving the response from the other person, "I'm fine, how are you?" whereupon you give the slightly embarrassing response, "I'm fine, how are you?" (Oops, already asked that—trapped in a feedback loop.) It isn't common sense that necessitates such implicit rules. It's personal preferences and cultural norms.

Given the value differences between individualist and collectivist cultures already discussed, it should come as no surprise that rules of appropriateness vary widely among cultures. Consider approaches to job interviews. Applicants in highly individualist cultures such as the United States are expected to engage in *self-enhancement* by initiating job searches and overtly promoting themselves just short of outright boasting. In most collectivist countries, however, applicants are expected to manifest *self-effacement*, which minimizes their accomplishments to show modesty especially by using self-deprecating messages.[19] Self-enhancing communication can seem abrasive and repel employers who expect self-effacement, and self-effacing communication can seem timid and ineffectual to employers who expect self-enhancement.

Even what is considered appropriate regarding mundane behavior can vary markedly among cultures. For example, in Japan, South Korea, New Zealand, China, and Costa Rica, tipping is frowned on because you are communicating the offensive message that the waitperson requires a bribe to provide acceptable service. In Egypt, tipping is permitted but a bit complicated. There are attendants at most public restrooms, especially those primarily available for tourists, and some staff provide toilet paper based on the size of the advance tip.[20] The awkwardness of this cultural difference I leave to your imagination.

There is an expectation that rules will be followed, but when rules are violated by inappropriate behavior, the results can be consequential. *Rules, however, are not immutable.* Some may be relaxed even though common sense may initially deem some rule changes as inadvisable. One study found that viewing cat videos on YouTube while at work reduces stress and can enhance employee performance and productivity if done occasionally.[21]

Effectiveness is the second principal element of the communication competence definition. *Effectiveness* is the degree to which individuals or groups have progressed toward the achievement of their goals. Goals, however, may not always be achievable. Your lack of effectiveness may be due to circumstances beyond your control. An individual can exhibit commendable, absolutely appropriate communication and still have relationships fail. There may be personality clashes, inept communication, and venal behavior instigated by others. Nevertheless, a pattern of relationship failures suggests deficiencies.

Effectiveness is contextual. You may be proficient at establishing strong relationships with most coworkers, but you may feel uncomfortable in large gatherings of strangers at parties. You may have a friend who looks forward to the challenge of delivering a presentation to a large audience, while you would rather be dipped in molasses and strapped to an anthill than give such a speech. Communication competence can vary by degrees from highly proficient to severely deficient depending on the circumstances. No one is a perfect communicator.

Because communication is transactional, effectiveness is more likely when focusing on "We" (what makes relationships and groups effective), not "Me" (what puts individual needs and goals as primary at the expense of others). Too often, however, the Me orientation, not the We orientation, seems commonsensical, especially in an individualist culture such as the United States that tends to emphasize the Me at the expense of the We. For example, Nathan Miller asserts that "conversation in the United States is a competitive exercise in which the first person to draw a breath is declared the listener."[22] This poor listening has been dubbed *conversational narcissism*—the tendency of listeners "to turn the topics of ordinary conversations to themselves without showing sustained interest in others' topics."[23] "Well, I've been talking long enough about me, so what do you think of me" encapsulates the conversational narcissist.[24] J. B. Priestley commented on the reputed good listening abilities of the wife of playwright and egotist George Bernard Shaw, "God knows she had plenty of practice." Conversational narcissists are viewed as socially inept and incompetent communicators.[25]

Conversational narcissism is exhibited by an attention-*getting* initiative called the *shift response*, which is Me oriented. Conversely, the more constructive listening behavior called a *support response* is an attention-*giving*, We-oriented cooperative effort by the listener to focus attention on the other person, not on oneself.[26] Consider examples that highlight differences between shift and support responses:

> Esperanza: I'm feeling very frustrated that we have accomplished al-
> most nothing.
> Maddox: I was more frustrated by most team members' Internet surf-
> ing during our meeting yesterday. Let's discuss that. (*shift response*)

Notice that Maddox ignores Esperanza's frustration. Instead, she shifts the focus to her own frustration. Now see the difference when a support response rather than a shift response occurs:

> Esperanza: I'm feeling very frustrated that we have accomplished al-
> most nothing.
> Maddox: Me too. What do you think we should do about it? (*support response*)

Here, the response from the listener keeps the focus on the speaker.

The shift response may be effective in some instances in which individuals drift from the main topic of conversation like hot-air balloons caught in a sudden updraft that requires a course correction. Research shows, however, that conversational narcissism is widespread in marriages and correlates strongly with divorce.[27] Therefore, emphasize support responses and use shift responses infrequently. *Background acknowledgment* ("yes," "OK"), a *supportive assertion* ("That's great," "Well done"), and a *supportive question* ("How do you think we should manage this?") are examples of supportive responses that encourage active listening and cooperative transactions, not competitive wrestling for attention.

The importance of the We orientation stretches beyond just listening. Psychologist Dacher Keltner[28] concludes, based on voluminous scientific studies, that constructive power and influence in business and organizations depend on putting "the focus on others," not on oneself. Research reveals that the number one reason workers are unhappy is because of bad bosses who exhibit less interest in the welfare of employees than in nailing a good tee time on the golf links.[29] Be audience centered not self-centered. This may seem like mere common sense, but it is far more difficult to recognize what communication behaviors work and what do not, and to implement constructive communication even if you have an inkling about what should be done.

3

MYTH: SKILL BUILDING IS KEY TO COMMUNICATION SUCCESS

Type "communication skills" into an Internet search window and up pops an abundance of articles touting a seemingly random number of such skills ranging from 5 to 25 that are purportedly critical to success, especially in the workplace. *Forbes* magazine offers a typical example titled: "8 Tips for Better Communication Skills."[1] In short paragraphs, the article delineates the following skill set: be clear and concise, prepare ahead of time, be mindful of nonverbal communication, watch your tone, practice active listening, build your emotional intelligence, develop a workplace communication strategy, and create a positive organizational culture. Entire books have been written about most of these skills, but superficial articles similar to this one appear frequently on the Internet from various supposed experts on communication. *Equating skill building alone with competent communication is just a myth, a gross misrepresentation of the difficulties and challenges inherent in striving to achieve such a result.*

Skill building isolated from the complex nature of competent communication serves little purpose. It is like learning the skills of how to crack an egg without breaking the yolk, effective ways to chop onions without slicing off a finger, learning to sauté vegetables without turning them into lumps of carbon, knowing how to cook pasta without transforming it into mush, and mastering how to make a roux (look it up) without it clumping. These are useful cooking skills, but in aggregate they won't ensure a delicious meal or make you a competent chef. Likewise, so much more is involved in communicating competently than just skill building.

In fact, *learning isolated communication skills can prove to be harmful in some situations.* For example, confrontation—directly addressing a conflict with others in an effort to resolve differences—is an appropriate and effective strategy for dealing with interpersonal conflict generally (see Chapter 13). It is, however, the worst strategy that a stalking victim can choose because it feeds a stalker's unquenchable desire for contact, any contact, with the victim.[2] In a leadership position, developing decisiveness can be a refreshing communication behavior when a team is accustomed to frustrating indecisiveness. Indiscriminate decisiveness, however, may prove harmful to team cooperation and problem-solving without a sophisticated understanding and appreciation for complicated causes of group challenges. Is leader decisiveness employed for constructive or destructive purposes? It matters. Learning persuasive speaking skills can be used for altruistic purposes or for advocating hatred and promoting prejudice and violence. As I will soon discuss, ethics matters.

So, isolated skill building does not equal communication competence. Effectiveness and appropriateness are the two key elements of communication competence, and you need to achieve both. To accomplish this, you begin with knowledge, not with skill building devoid of knowledge. *Knowledge* provides a foundation for understanding what is required for communication proficiency. We cannot determine what is appropriate and effective without knowing the rules operating in a specific context. When hired for a new job, for example, you learn to navigate based on apparent rules. Should you address your boss formally or casually? Is there a dress code? Can you tease your supervisor, or will this get you moved to a job equivalent to cleaning up after elephants following a circus parade? These are only some rules that you should discover at your workplace depending on your position.

Knowledge of certain rules can be especially important. For example, Canela Lopez and Marquerite Ward identify a dozen remarks to avoid saying to LGBTQ+ coworkers. These include the following: (1) never offer a "compliment" by saying "You don't strike me as gay"; (2) do not keep mentioning your one gay family member; and (3) avoid saying, "I would never have guessed you were transgender."[3] Rules are changing concerning gender identity, so remaining current in your knowledge is important if you hope to avoid appearing insensitive and offensive.

The misconceived focus on skill building alone, however, does not mean that skills are unimportant. Knowledge absent skill is knowing how without showing how to communicate competently. Skill puts your knowledge into practice. A *communication skill* is the ability to perform a communication behavior effectively and repeatedly. Knowledge and skill are integral partners. Knowing what you should do to interview successfully for a job will not automatically secure the position. You can know all the perfect answers to interview questions, but if you cannot articulate those answers without repetitive distracting vocal disfluencies such as "um," "ah," "like," and "you know," then failure is almost assured.

Even knowledge and skill are insufficient for competent communication to take place. You also need sensitivity. *Sensitivity* means receptive accuracy—the ability to detect, decode, and decipher signals from others.[4] Emotional intelligence (see Chapter 1) is a key part of exhibiting sensitivity. Can you tell when a friend is uncomfortable, shy, angry, or just awkward? When your boss frowns during a meeting, is this person showing confusion, taking offense, disagreeing, or suddenly remembering the dog was left alone in the house with no exit for using the outdoors as a toilet? Accurately decoding both verbal and nonverbal messages is not always obvious and may require seeking clarification (does your boss even own a dog?). Research reveals that *listeners are emotionally attuned to a speaker's message less than 5% of the time.*[5] If you don't attend to the signals that indicate other people's emotional needs because you aren't focusing, then you can miss connecting meaningfully with those who can make life a joyful experience.

Communication knowledge, skill building, and sensitivity to emotional needs of others also require *commitment*, that passion for excellence that compels us to improve. Commitment is exhibited in tandem with sensitivity by *mindfulness* when "we think about our communication and continually work at changing what we do in order to become more effective."[6] We exhibit *mindlessness* when we drift through life oblivious to our communication and its effects on others or we simply don't care, and consequently we put little or no effort into improving it. Attitude and aptitude are equally important. The predominant motivation of the competent communicator is the dogged desire to avoid repeating the same mistakes and to find better ways of communicating with others.

Finally, unlike the beasts-as-feasts daily killing field that takes place among animals on the African Serengeti, we humans value the difference between right and wrong behavior (appropriateness). *Ethics* is a set of moral standards for judging what constitutes that right and wrong behavior. The National Communication Association promotes five ethical communication standards.[7] Honesty (truthfulness), respect (due regard for feelings and rights of others), fairness (equal treatment), choice (freedom from coercion), and responsibility (accountability for our actions) are the key elements.

In the abstract, these five ethical standards may seem unambiguous and noncontroversial, but they can clash at times. For example, brutal honesty that savages a person's self-esteem ignores emotional intelligence and respect for the well-being of others. Where is the sensitivity in telling a person that they are unattractive for the sake of blunt honesty? Consider *ethnocentrism*—exalting one's own culture while disparaging other cultures based on differences in practices, behaviors, and beliefs used as standards of evaluation. This is prejudice on a global scale. Unfortunately, ethnocentrism permeates all cultures to greater or lesser extent.[8]

Although ethnocentrism is cultural prejudice, that does not mean that cultural values and beliefs are inviolable and should be accepted blindly. To respect a culture's beliefs even when it promotes dehumanization collides with standards of respect for contrary beliefs, fairness, and choice. Ethnocentrism cannot be countered with the superficial justification, "That's just the way they do things in their culture." Despite such complexities, however, all five ethical standards—honesty, respect, fairness, choice, and responsibility—are strong values in our culture that closely parallel the United Nations

Universal Declaration of Human Rights,[9] and serve as important guidelines for our communication competence.

To summarize briefly, a skills-only view of communication competence is a myth. We achieve communication competence, not merely by building an array of isolated skills (e.g., assertiveness, sophisticated vocabulary, persuasive delivery of messages) but also by mastering the complex interrelationships among knowledge, skills, sensitivity, commitment, and ethics. Anything less just promotes a disquietingly shallow, even dangerous view of human communication.

④

MYTH: COMMUNICATE MORE FOR SUCCESS GALORE

"**O**ne of our culture's most cherished ideas is that when it comes to communication in relationships, more is better."[1] This is a myth.[2] Communication quantity often does not equal communication quality. More verbal abuse, dishonesty, rumor dissemination, incessant criticism and judgment, dogmatism, arrogance, clumsy presentations, and inept or even hurtful approaches to addressing conflict in relationships hardly improve our communication with others by increasing their amount. You'd have to be masochistic to want more of that kind of communication. "The words you choke back, the fights you never start, and the pointless criticisms that never see the light of day will be the heroes of your personal and professional relationships."[3] Sometimes less is more.

Advanced technologies have given us a multitude of media to communicate with others. This isn't axiomatically a constructive experience. With such technologies comes the challenge of not becoming overwhelmed by the barrage of constant, easily accessible communication that is not always welcome or constructive. One study of 14,000 employees and business leaders in 17 countries revealed that 78% are getting bombarded with much more communication from many more sources than ever.[4] Another study by Grammarly Business based on a Harris poll concludes: "Today's hybrid workplace is a whirlwind of communication. Quantity has increased, but quality is declining."[5]

Technology entrepreneur Mitchell Kapor once noted, "Getting information off the Internet is like taking a drink from a fire hydrant." The pervasive use of increasingly powerful Swiss Army knife–like smartphones exacerbates the problem. The CRAY-2 supercomputer in 1985 became the fastest and most powerful machine ever built. By comparison, smartphones of today are more than 5,000 times faster. If the CRAY-2 were as powerful as the iPhone 12, it would take up a staggering 80,000 square feet and weigh a prodigious 27.5 million pounds.[6] The power of smartphones continues to advance even further since this assessment. Add to this the rise of ChatGPT and advances in artificial intelligence, which may be a help or hindrance, or both, as yet to be definitively determined. Electronic technology has created the age of information overload that complicates our communication with other people.

Information overload incontrovertibly counters the myth that being ever more accessible to others as a result of technological advances in communication media automatically means more communication is better communication. Aside from feeling buried by the avalanche of information, there are *several significant consequences of information overload.*

1. *Inattention to Tasks.* The average "knowledge worker" compulsively checks emails and instant messages every 6 minutes.[7] These email interruptions divert workers' attention from their normal tasks for more than 90 minutes a day, on average.[8]
2. *Impaired Thinking.* Jonathon Spira, director of the Information Overload Research Group, states, "Information overload causes people to lose their ability to manage thoughts and ideas, contemplate, and even reason and think."[9] Research discovered that mental capacity is diminished by an average of 10 IQ points, comparable to missing a night's sleep, by persistent emailing and text messaging.[10] The easy availability of gigaheaps of information can overwhelm our capacity for analyzing information critically. Who has the time to think when a massive amount of information bombards us?

3. *Decision Hesitance.* With technological advances, faster has become the common expectation. Psychologist Philip Zimbardo comments on this "need for speed": "Technology makes us impatient for anything that takes more than seconds to achieve. You press a button and you expect instant access."[11] One study of workers found that 70% have given up on making some decisions because the data is overwhelming.[12]

4. *Creativity Curtailment.* When our minds are cluttered with a massive mound of mundane information, not just critical thinking but also creative thinking is greatly impeded.[13] A "quieter mind yields more creative ideas."[14] It is difficult to focus on creative solutions to challenging problems when the distraction of too much worthless information interferes.

So how does one cope with information overload? There are several ways.[15]

1. *Filter Information.* Be hyper-selective when sifting through information to find what deserves your attention and what should be ignored. This may require nothing beyond a quick scan of the topic and author of electronic messages.

2. *Halt Social Media Cruising.* Put yourself on a social media diet and reduce the digital distractions. Some companies have established quiet times. Communicating electronically is prohibited to give employees time to think and problem-solve and to meet in groups and make decisions. One study found that preventing dissemination of e-mail for five days resulted in group members increasing face-to-face communication, and participants were more focused on tasks and less distracted by attempts to multitask.[16]

3. *Stop Multitasking.* You may think you can concentrate on two competing stimuli simultaneously, but you can't.[17] As comedian Doug Benson amusingly relates: "Just the other day I was walking down the street, I was putting eyedrops in my eyes, I was talking on my cellphone, and I was getting hit by a car." Substantial research clearly shows that multitasking decreases performance.[18] Psychologist Clifford Nass summarizes the mul-

titasking problem this way: "It turns out multitaskers are terrible at every aspect of multitasking. They're terrible at ignoring irrelevant information; they're terrible at keeping information in their head nicely and neatly organized; and they're terrible at switching from one task to another."[19]

4. *Be Selective*. This distinguishes what we need to know from what there is to know. You need to find the few gold nuggets among the slag heap of look-alike iron pyrite or "fool's gold" of useless information. Set priorities. Once priorities have been determined, useless from useful information can be ascertained.

5. *Limit the Search*. Setting deadlines for individual or group decisions is crucial. Deadlines force you to halt the search for information, which could go on interminably. This means, however, that the search for information should not be delayed.

In brief summary, communication quantity does not equal quality. More communication is not always desirable. More competent communication is.

⑤

MYTH: COMMUNICATION IS A MAGIC ELIXIR

Learning to communicate competently is essential to developing and sustaining interpersonal and group relationships. Sources of friction in personal relationships, however, can't always be fixed by improving communication even when it is exemplary. Sometimes communicating clearly reveals just how far apart individuals have grown. Your coworker may always have a sour disposition and a cynical view of the political landscape. Your boss may never be more than an inconsiderate, power-grubbing tyrant. Your roommate may never become less than a hygienic disaster. Improving your interviewing skills is important to your employment future, but it won't help land a high-skills, professional position if the most challenging aspect of any job you've held involved asking, "Would you like fries with that?" Your odds of landing such a position is about the same as a snail's safe passage across a freeway at rush hour. You need to expand your résumé.

Competent communication can provide means of coping effectively with diverse challenges, but it may not change people's behavior in the ways we might wish. Clear, honest communication may reveal irreconcilable differences. Adept communication may ease the pain of breaking up, but its lingering effects may remain even years later.

Improving communication is not a magic elixir. Organizations, for example, may be dysfunctional because of systemic problems beyond an individual's control. If workers' roles and responsibilities are confusing, and opportunities for sound decision-making and problem-solving are remote due to a top-down hierarchical power distribution, then skillful communication by those in weak positions of power to make such changes won't likely improve a dysfunctional system. Even training employees to improve their communication in such a counterproductive system will likely prove futile without structural changes.[1] Jettisoning individuals who are uncooperative or disruptive may prove to be more constructive than mandating dubiously effective weekend "team building" training sessions that end with "happy sheets" or "smiley-face" evaluations of the "ropes course" or zip line activities.[2] Sometimes teams disintegrate because members don't like each other or because they have contradictory visions for the group aside from the quality of the group's communication. *Communication is a means to an end, but not an end in itself.* Every relationship problem cannot be cured by improving your communication because not all such problems emanate from deficient communication.

Just because communication competence is not a cure-all for every relationship difficulty, however, does not mean that communication improvement is insignificant. Research reveals that competent communication is essential for success in business and the workplace.[3] One survey of almost 1,000 employers from 628 companies in 51 countries listed effective oral communication as the most desirable skill for employees to possess, followed by listening skills, written communication, and presentation skills. Technical and administrative skills appeared way down the list.[4] Another extensive study by LinkedIn of 100 metropolitan areas in the United States reported that competent communication is the most highly desirable employee ability.[5] Students likewise recognize the importance of communication competence for "career readiness."[6] The importance of effective communication on successful interpersonal relationships is also strongly supported by copious research.[7] Remember, however, that skill development alone is insufficient. Skills without knowledge, sensitivity, commitment, and ethics ignores context and the interrelationships among all elements of appropriate and effective communication.

Developing communication competence is not a one-and-done process. It is a lifelong enterprise that requires agility to roll with constant change and persistent updating to remain relevant and effective as our world changes and new challenges emerge, sometimes surprisingly so. For example, consider the massively disruptive, unexpected communication challenges and frequently inept attempts to adapt to the COVID-19 pandemic! Even managing the "mute" option on Zoom often seemed too difficult. "You're muted . . . Still muted." More significantly, companies and small businesses had to be flexible or perish. As the authors of *Out of Office* explain, flexibility "means reconceiving what sorts of tasks and collaborations need to be synchronous [occurring in person] and what can actually be done asynchronously [virtually], and how many days we'd like people to be in an office, and for how long, and for what purpose."[8]

Communication competence is not a cure-all, but inept communication can be a ticket to disaster. Learning to communicate appropriately and effectively can significantly improve your chances of successful outcomes even though some problems may remain despite your best efforts and communication proficiency.

6

MYTH: MEANINGS ARE IN WORDS

A friend of mine told me this story about his daughter Janie, who was five years old at the time. Janie was playing with a boy in the neighborhood who was about the same age. Something this little boy did made Janie very angry. She turned to the him and yelled, "I'm going to shit on your head." Janie's mom heard her daughter's outburst and immediately reprimanded her, "Janie, we don't talk like that." Janie seemed a little confused but then said to the boy, "I'm going to shit on your arm."

Janie's mom unmistakenly had a strong negative reaction to Janie's surprising foray into the world of offensive language. *Denotation*—shared meaning of a word usually found in a dictionary—doesn't seem to be the real issue. The objectionable word was viewed as inoffensive for centuries in England before becoming taboo in the early part of the 19th century.[1] Would Janie's mom have been so alarmed if Janie instead had said, "I'm going to toidee on your head"? She might have admonished Janie while trying to stifle a chuckle. If the objectively neutral denotative meaning were producing the emphatic, negative reaction, then why can a doctor ask you for a *feces* or *stool* sample without inviting censure? The denotation of all three words is identical—namely, excrement—yet the *connotation*—personal meaning for a word gained through associations and experiences—is not. To clarify the difference between denotation and connotation, consider the word *mother*. It denotes a female parent but may connote warmth, admiration, affection, or fear, loathing, and hostility depending on your field of experiences.

Negative reaction to "obscene words" is a learned behavior. What is offensive to one person may be amusing to another. Janie's dad chuckled when he told me about his daughter's use of verbal obscenity, even though I never heard him use any taboo terms aside from when he told the story about his daughter. Words such as *virgin*, *slut*, *tart*, *sex*, *pregnant*, and *virtuous* were all censored from U.S. newspapers and motion pictures until the latter half of the 20th century.[2] Timidity concerning openly communicating about sex ruled. By today's standards, viewing these words as offensive seems silly. It was not the denotations for these words that provoked the ban. It was the connotations, the learned associations attached to the words that triggered the prohibitions. Constantly being told from early childhood that "We don't talk like that" reinforces linguistic taboos.

Janie didn't seem aware that she had used a "bad word." She apparently thought that the location of the threatened act was cause for concern, and there is some logic in viewing the head as more objectionable than the arm for the threatened act. Janie's mom exhibited a mistaken view that some words are just inherently obscene and offensive, or she at least worried that other people might have thought so. *No word, however, is "naturally" obscene*. A word does not get deemed obscene or offensive because of some inherent meaning, but individuals and groups often act as though this isn't obvious. Ethnic slurs, oaths, slogans, chants, and buzzwords in advertising and politics can ignite *signal reactions*—an automatic, unthinking, emotional response to words that seem to impute inherent meaning to the words themselves. Words, and their function in all languages, do not gain meaning apart from their associations in a context and culture. *Bollocks* is a swear word in Britain, but to Americans you might as well have said *fumadiddle* for all the impact that it evokes. Every culture has some words that are considered vulgar or taboo, but if you don't speak the language and have cultural associations with the offensive terms, then the words are just meaningless noise.[3]

To further elaborate beyond offensive or emotive terms, the operating rule for all words as the building blocks of language and as a medium for sharing meaning is this: *word origin is arbitrary, but word usage is conventional.* An *automobile* could be arbitrarily called a *poncentrot*, a word I made up as I was typing this sentence. If the English-using community, however, does not embrace my invented word and its meaning, it will disappear with little or no notice, which I confidently expect. Word meanings rely on conventionality or common agreement, not natural law. Shakespeare originated more than 1,700 words such as *barefoot, critical, submerged,* and yes, *obscene,* but *barky, brisky, tortive,* and *vastidity* were some that failed to gain conventionality.[4]

Taking this a bit further, *sniglets,* a term invented by comedian Rich Hall, refers to words that he asserts should be in a dictionary but are not. They illustrate the arbitrariness of word origin and its sometimes transitory result.[5] Here are a few examples: *arachnidiot* (an individual who, having stumbled into an "invisible" spiderweb, begins windmilling their arms and flailing wildly); *textpectation* (the anticipation experienced when waiting for a response to a text); *cellfish* (an individual who continues talking on their cellphone when doing so is rude or inconsiderate of other people); *doork* (a person who pushes on a door clearly marked "pull"), and *aquadextrous* (possessing the ability to turn the bathtub faucet with your toes). None of these "made-up words," however, will have meaning and become part of the English *lexicon*—total vocabulary—without conventionality, our common agreement to use these words with these specific meanings. Their meaning is not embedded in the words themselves.

As a speech community, English speakers tacitly agree to certain meanings and appropriate usages for words, even if this sometimes seems odd, even illogical. For example, why can you drive in *park*ways but park in *drive*ways? Why are *jail* and *prison* synonyms, but *jailer* and *prisoner* are antonyms? The simple answer is that when decoding words, we give them agreed-upon meanings even if it doesn't seem strictly logical.

Common agreement can be tricky when cultures whose principal native language is not English are involved. Electrolux, a Scandinavian company, discovered this when promoting its vacuum cleaners in the United States with the advertising slogan "Nothing sucks like an Electrolux." Cringeworthy translations on English signs throughout Beijing during its turn hosting the Olympics had to be swiftly corrected. "Deformed Man Toilet" was thankfully changed to the at least somewhat improved "Disabled Person Toilet," and "Beijing Anus Hospital" was fortunately altered to "Beijing Proctology Hospital."[6]

Word meanings are not immutable. Meanings can change, and they often do, producing the challenge of accurately deciphering them when there are multiple meanings of words, demonstrated by the famous quip by Groucho Marx, "Time flies like an arrow; fruit flies like a banana." Similarly, Robert C. Gallagher remarks, "Change is inevitable, except from a vending machine." Then there are actual newspaper headlines reported by the *Columbia Journalism Review*: "Teacher Strikes Idle Kids"; "Miners Refuse to Work After Death"; "Panda Mating Fails—Veterinarian Takes Over" and "City Manager Tapes Head to District Attorney." Imagine a nonnative speaker of English trying to decode this sentence: "The woman was present to present the present to her boss, presently." Lexicographer Peter Gilliver determined that the word *run* has 645 distinct meanings, making it the definitional champion in the English language. You can run a mile, engage in a trial run, have a run of bad luck, run an app on your smartphone, and no, I'm not going to list all 645 meanings, but you can project the possibilities.[7] Then there is the challenge of deciphering words that can have contradictory meanings, called *contronyms*, such as *clip* (fasten or cut away), *garnish* (add to food or take away wages), *fast* (move quickly or stick firmly), and *blunt* (dull instrument or sharp, pointed remark).

Even when "sharing" a common native language across cultures, problems can arise. For example, *boot* to the British is a trunk to Americans. A *biscuit* is a cookie, *pants* are not trousers but underwear, a *purse* is a wallet, and *crisps* are the equivalent of American potato chips. George Bernard Shaw once remarked that England and America are two countries separated by the same language.

Words are the building blocks of language. They are organic. We invent new words as needed (drug companies do so regularly when labeling every new medication with often tongue-twisting names— Xgeva, Xeljanz, Idarucizumab, Qtern), and we play with words. A *portmanteau*—a term for the blending of two or more words or parts of words that expresses some combination of the meaning of its parts—is an apt example. *Smog* was an early example that combined smoke and fog. *Brunch* (from breakfast and lunch), *hangry* (from hungry and angry), *glamping* (glamorous + camping); and *Barbenheimer* (combination of the two massive hit movies titled *"Barbie"* and *"Oppenheimer"* released simultaneously in 2023) are additional examples. We can play with words and their meanings because they are *symbols*—arbitrary representations of objects, events, ideas, or relationships of our own creation. Thus, what should by now be abundantly clear is that word meanings are in us, not in the words themselves.

7

MYTH: SIGN LANGUAGE IS NOT A REAL LANGUAGE, BUT BODY LANGUAGE IS

Noted neurologist Oliver Sacks, responding to the plight of individuals who experience the loss of language understanding and usage from Alzheimer's disease, calls the resultant language deficiency "one of the most desperate of calamities, for it is only through language that we enter fully into our human estate and culture, communicate freely with our fellows, acquire and share information."[1] Psycholinguist Steven Pinker echoes this view: "Language is so tightly woven into human experience that it is scarcely possible to imagine life without it."[2] In the next chapter, I explore more specifically the power of human language to influence our thinking, perception, and behavior. But before such exploration, what exactly is language, and do sign language and body language really qualify? This is not a mere esoteric exercise. As I will show, there are consequences to designating any communication code as a language. Entire academic disciplines, such as linguistics and its psycholinguistics and sociolinguistics offshoots, intensely study what constitutes language and how it functions as a means of human communication.

To the casual observer, sign language may appear to be akin to charades or merely a series of *iconic* representations that mimic objects or actions related to segments of speech, such as typing on a keyboard in the air with finger gestures or moving your hand toward your mouth as if eating. Conversely, body language is a form of nonverbal communication that uses physical movements to convey messages and often accompanies verbal communication. Whether either of these two forms of communication are actual languages requires knowing what qualifies as a language, and that is not a simple endeavor, as will become obvious.

Language is a structured system of symbols for communicating meaning. There are approximately 7,100 spoken languages in the world.[3] At first glance, they may seem markedly different from each other. Native speakers of English undoubtedly struggle to mimic the sounds of Mandarin, Arabic, Japanese, Xhosa, Swahili, or Bengali, and understanding such languages takes lots of practice. Despite such apparent differences, *all languages have four common characteristics: structure, productivity, displacement, and self-reflexiveness.*

Structure is the most vital element of any language, and it is far and away the most complicated. *If a communication code has no structure, it is not a language.* Grammar structures meaningful expression of messages in every language. *Grammar* is the set of rules that dictates how the units of language—phonemes, morphemes, phrases, and sentences—can be meaningfully constructed.

Phonemes are the individual units of sound that comprise a spoken language. These phonemes correspond to vowels (*a, e, i, o, u*), consonants (such as *b, c, d, x, y, z*), and consonant combinations called *digraphs* (*cl, fr, gr, pl, sh, th*). No single language encompasses more than a fraction of the myriad noises that people can produce—some lewd, crude, and rude. Linguists have identified 3,183 distinct phonemes in 2,186 languages studied. English, however, has only 40–44 phonemes (varies depending on a speaker's accent); the Hawaiian language has a mere 13, and the African language !Xoo has 158.[4]

Every language has separate phonological rules determining which phonemes correspond to which languages, how to pronounce these sounds, and how to combine phonemes in meaningful ways. These rules "find order within the apparent chaos of speech sounds."[5] They also can vary widely across the many different languages spoken around the globe. For example, unlike English, in the Czech language complete sentences can be composed without any vowels, such as the common tongue twister *strc prst skrz krk* ("stick a finger through your throat").[6]

Phonemes are combined to create morphemes, which allow humans to communicate in more sophisticated ways than is possible by primitive grunting, snorting, and pointing. A *morpheme* is the smallest unit of meaning in a language. Morphemes are not just words. A morpheme can be a stand-alone word (*chain*) labeled a *free morpheme*, or it can be a *bound morpheme* that has no meaning until it is attached to a stand-alone word. Examples of bound morphemes include prefixes such as *un* in *unchain* or suffixes such as *ing* in *unchaining* and *s* as in *chains* that pluralizes nouns.

As humans, we combine words (morphemes) into phrases ("the long, cool woman in a black dress") and phrases into sentences ("She is the long, cool woman in a black dress"). We do this based on grammatical rules called *syntax*. "Workers lifted the steel girders" is a meaningful sentence, but "Lifted girders workers steel the" is not. Why? The rule is that an article (*the*) and adjective (*steel*) come before the noun (*girders*), and the verb (*lifted*) follows the subject (*workers*). Subject-verb-object (SVO) is, syntactically, the standard English word order. This standard order is why the speech of Yoda, the Jedi Master in the *Star Wars* films, sounds so odd. Yodaspeak, such as "Pain, suffering, and death I feel" and "Found someone, you have?" exhibit an object-subject-verb (OSV) order that is very unusual for English and almost all other world languages.[7]

Communicating meaning in English is highly dependent on word-order rules. Groucho Marx famously made this very point: "One morning I shot an elephant in my pajamas. How he got in my pajamas I'll never know." This is called a misplaced modifier, a violation of a standard word-order rule. The sentence should read, "While in my pajamas, I shot an elephant." The sentences "Skateboarding is not a crime" and "Not skateboarding is a crime" have the same words but certainly don't have the same meaning. Word order rules are important because they provide structure for communicating meaning, but not all languages have the same ones.

Productivity—the limitless capacity of language to transform a small number of phonemes into whatever words, phrases, and sentences are required to share your copious thoughts and feelings—is the second essential element of language besides structure.[8] New words sprout up like mushrooms in loamy soil to identify new products, scientific discoveries, abstract concepts and ideas, and technologies (ChatGPT is a recent creation). Global Language Monitor estimates that roughly 15 words in English are invented *each day*.[9] Remember, however, that word origin is arbitrary and word usage is conventional, as discussed in the previous chapter. Absent common usage, invented words drift into oblivion. Some words enter the language and then eventually disappear from lack of usage. For example, *sluberdegullion* (slovenly), *houppelande* (cloak), *snoutfair* (surprisingly, it meant an attractive person), and *beef-witted* (can you guess? It meant stupid) have disappeared.[10]

Productivity allows us to communicate with extraordinarily creative variety. This last sentence clearly isn't Shakespeare, but it is almost assuredly an original creation (and, yes, I gave it a Google check). Considering just grammatically correct six-word sentences, there are approximately 1 million possibilities. Increase that to 20-word sentences, and there are an incredible *100 million trillion possibilities*.[11] As linguist David Adger notes, "If you make up a sentence of any complexity, and search for the exact sentence on the Internet, it's almost never there. Virtually everything we say is novel."[12]

The third essential element of a language is *displacement*—your ability to use language to talk about objects, ideas, events, and relations that don't just exist in the physical here and now.[13] You can communicate about things that don't exist, such as unicorns, fairies, hobbits, and corporate responsibility. You can discuss past experiences or future hoped-for accomplishments. You can ask questions about only imagined, even bizarre things, such as "If an alien had three legs instead of just two, could they run faster than a human, or would they simply trip and fall on their two faces?" You can contemplate abstract ideas, such as this bumper sticker "logic": "I'm nobody, nobody is perfect, therefore I'm perfect" or comedian Steven Wright's query: "If you are in a spaceship that is traveling at the speed of light, and you turn on the headlights, does anything happen?" The displacement capacity of language helps us all learn from previous mistakes and ponder potential solutions for anticipated future problems. Language gives each of us the ability to share messages about the past, present, or future; about things that may exist, don't exist, or can't exist; about the imaginary and ethereal as well as the concrete and physical.

The final essential element of a language is its *self-reflexiveness*—the capacity to use language to talk about language.[14] Every language has the capacity to be self-reflexive. This discussion is an example of self-reflexiveness. I am using English to analyze and discuss both English and languages in general, using a vocabulary that has been developed to identify and discuss the nature of languages (e.g., phonemes, morphemes, syntax) and ways to improve its use to accomplish important goals.

Considering all four essential elements of language—structure, productivity, displacement, and self-reflexiveness—do sign languages qualify? Yes, they do, despite the prevalent myth noted by neurologist Oliver Sacks that sign languages are mistakenly seen as "something rudimentary, primitive, pantomimic, a poor thing."[15] Most signs, like words in spoken languages, are arbitrary representations of their *referents*—what they refer to.[16] The signs have no inherent meaning apart from human interpretation. *Sign origin is arbitrary; sign usage is conventional.* Unlike pantomime, most signs in American Sign Language (ASL) and any of the more than 300 other sign languages, such as British (BSL) or Japanese (JSL) versions, are *not iconic.* Thus, the various versions of sign languages are not mutually intelligible.[17] Users of JSL or even BSL, for example, will not understand ASL users in conversation because these are languages each with their own arbitrary constellation of signs and even different grammatical rules. There is also Black American Sign Language (BASL), which is considered a dialect, or variety, of ASL not always intelligible to ASL-only users. BASL uses more facial expressions and two hands for a sign where ASL users employ just a single hand, and some signs are completely different when comparing ASL and BASL.[18]

"American Sign Language (ASL) is a complete language that has the same linguistic properties as spoken languages, with grammar that differs from English."[19] In fact, "You can change the syntax with a shrug, a frown, a smile, a nod, or a turn to the left or right."[20] Every sign language is a structured system of symbols that can be expanded (productivity) to incorporate any thought or feeling—concrete or abstract, immediate or far away, real or imaginary (displacement)—and sign languages can use signs to discuss signs (self-reflexiveness). Viewing any sign language as mere pantomime diminishes its significance as a complicated means of human communication, and it consequentially diminishes its users as capable of using only a primitive means of communicating. This is an egregiously dehumanizing myth that significantly devalues the remarkable linguistic capabilities of the Deaf community.

Unlike sign language, "body language" is a misnomer. In an article titled "Body Language Analysis in Healthcare," Rawad Abdulghafor and associates make the mistaken claim in their first sentence, "Body language constitutes one of the languages of communication."[21] No, it doesn't. That's a myth. Calling nonverbal communication a language doesn't make it so. Interestingly, the article's authors note a few sentences later, "Body language is entirely different from sign language—a complete language—with its own basic rules and complex grammar system."

What has been labeled "body language" is not a language. It is a form of nonverbal communication that usually accompanies verbal communication, and nonverbal signals may change the verbally expressed meaning of a message; however, it lacks the essential elements that define languages. Most important, so-called body language has no structure. There is no body language grammar.[22] You don't have nonverbal sentences that require grammatical structure to produce meaning. When communicating happiness, a smile does not have to come before an eye raise, a hand gesture, or any other nonverbal cue. There simply is no required order, no syntax. There also is no nonverbal lexicon, no dictionary of nonverbal signals as there is for sign languages. We don't communicate self-reflexively about nonverbal cues, and these cues are usually concrete not abstract ones, so they do not communicate meaning about that which does not exist, past, present, or future.

Designating nonverbal communication as a body "language" is not merely a benign metaphor, meaning superficially but not literally like a verbal language. According to psychologists and language experts, calling nonverbal communication *body language* "is actually damaging." It "wrongly implies a relatively invariant rule book by which to decode specific appearance cues and behaviors."[23] Popular books such as *How to Read a Person Like a Book* and hundreds of other titles and articles that followed made it appear that specific nonverbal cues almost invariably have very specific meanings. Two studies involving thousands of respondents from 75 countries found that most thought "liars avert their eyes" is a sure sign of deception.[24] Research by the Paul Ekman Group notes that there is no single nonverbal cue that reliably reveals deception.[25] This and similar misconceptions concerning the alleged precise meaning of individual nonverbal cues fostered by erroneously labeling such communication cues as a "language" has promulgated "a multimillion-dollar body-language industry in books, seminars, videos, and other media, dedicated to revealing the hidden codes and subtle strategies that are promised to ensure success in every aspect of social life . . . [but] consumers should be wary of claims that they can purchase access to any secret language of the body."[26] Calling gestures and other body activity a language is markedly imprecise and makes about as much sense as referencing the "language" of flowers, thorns, or trees, which happen to be book titles you can find on Amazon.

8

MYTH: 93% OF COMMUNICATION IS NONVERBAL

Jon Michail, in an article for *Forbes* magazine, asserts a common myth regarding the importance of nonverbal communication when he claims that "only 7% of all communication is done through verbal communication," leaving the remaining 93% to nonverbal elements. He even goes further by claiming that "nonverbal skills are even more important now than they were before this global pandemic (Covid)."[1] Management consultant Susan Heathfield makes this extraordinary claim, offering no qualifiers: "Nonverbal communication is the single most powerful form of communication."[2] She references the 93% statistic as support. Marketing consultant Ian Brodie notes the prevalence of this communication myth, "I've lost track of the number of times I've heard this [93% statistic] in sales training sessions or read it in books, articles and blogs."[3] As Joshua Uebergang, director of Digital Darts and business consultant, claims, the 93% statistic repeated ad nauseum "is a close contender for the greatest communication myth."[4]

Nonverbal communication is sharing meaning with others non-linguistically (without words, phrases, and sentences that require syntax). This excludes sign language that manually communicates linguistically (see Chapter 7). Countless Internet sites and even some communication textbooks misinterpret very narrow research conducted by Albert Mehrabian when they assert the 93% statistic.[5] Mehrabian's research consisted of female speakers uttering a single word in an inconsistent voice, with no context provided, and a judgment required about likability from a very small unrepresentative sample of student subjects. That's it! From this, Mehrabian concluded that 93% of the emotional meaning of this single word came from nonverbal cues such as tone of voice and facial expressions. Mehrabian never concluded that 93% of the meaning of all messages is determined nonverbally. In fact, he unequivocally repudiated it. In 2009, BBC reporter Tim Harford asked Mehrabian about this oft-repeated statistic. He replied: "Whenever I hear that misquote or misrepresentation of my findings I cringe because it should be so obvious to anybody who would use any amount of common sense that that's not the correct statement."[6]

The 93% statistic is nonsensical on its face when you consider, for example, watching a movie scene of two characters quarreling without the sound or closed captioning. Yes, you can realize that they are quarreling, and even correctly identify emotion exhibited (anger), but can you discern which one forgot to pick up milk on the way home, or who is fighting fair, or which person spent money the couple didn't have? Can you understand more than a mere hint of the meaning expressed during any interaction in China if you do not understand Mandarin or Cantonese? Can you imagine debating a philosophical question such as "What is the meaning of life?" mostly nonverbally? Try nonverbally communicating the complexities of science, history, psychology, high-level mathematics, or any of the myriad disciplines that comprise our educational system (including communication itself) with only scant use of language.

Learning a language, any language, becomes virtually irrelevant if only a minuscule 7% of meaning is derived from verbal communication. This is probably the strongest repudiation of the 93% myth. Minimizing language in this way grossly underestimates its prodigious power. I explored the power of language to influence thought, perception, and behavior extensively in other publications.[7] Here I provide just two examples to prove the point convincingly and dispel any lingering acceptance of the mistaken notion that only 7% of message meaning is derived from verbal communication. First, consider *framing*—the influence descriptive wording has on our perception. Note the differences in the following:

- *Wokeness* or *political correctness*
- *Global warming* or *climate change*
- *Undocumented immigrants* or *illegal aliens*
- *Adventurous activity* or *risky behavior*
- *90% surgical success rate* or *10% death rate*

Framing matters.[8] The frames we use with their accompanying narratives "determine whether people notice problems, how they understand and remember problems, and how they evaluate and act upon them."[9] Language frames influence viewpoints.[10]

The power of framing is supported by abundant research.[11] For example, when subjects read brief passages that described crime either as a "beast preying" on or as a "virus infecting" a city, those participants given the "beast" framing were inclined to choose punishment as the solution, but those presented with the "virus" framing were inclined to choose reform measures.[12] In another study, two groups were shown the same video of a protest in front of a building. When the video was labeled as an antiabortion protest at a health clinic, conservatives viewed it as a peaceful demonstration, but liberals saw protesters blocking the entrance and intimidating patients. When the video was shown to a second group and it was labeled as a protest against the exclusion of gay people at a military recruiting center, conservatives saw mayhem, but the liberals saw only a peaceful demonstration.[13]

A second example of the power of language is the use of verbal abuse that has severe consequences for targets of hurtful words. Verbal abuse of children, for example, is widespread and often devastatingly consequential. This verbal behavior "can be as damaging to a child's development as . . . childhood physical and sexual abuse."[14] Hurtful words from peers are also equivalent to parental verbal abuse in producing anxiety, depression, hostility, and drug use.[15] Such peer abuse has the added dimension of often appearing on the Internet, so "these very public insults and virtual assaults can 'go viral,' taking on lives of their own and persisting long after they would have otherwise lost their immediacy."[16]

Verbal abuse of nurses by doctors has become a serious national problem. From being told that "monkeys could be trained to do what nurses do" to being berated by a doctor, "You don't look dumber than my dog. Why can't you at least fetch what I need," verbal abuse of nurses by doctors has become epidemic.[17] A New York critical care nurse punctuated the pervasiveness of this problem, "Every single nurse I know has been verbally berated by a doctor. Every single one."[18] Verbal abuse by doctors unsurprisingly has consequences. The more frequent the verbal abuse, the greater the likelihood that the nurses will quit their jobs.[19] Patient care is also at risk as a result.[20]

With the advent of COVID-19, verbal abuse in the health care industry has taken on new depths of shocking treatment of health practitioners. One comprehensive study found that 68% of nurses reported verbal abuse and nearly as many reported physical abuse as well, mostly from out-of-control patients. Physicians also experienced similar verbal abuse.[21] Hospitals across the country, as a result of these survey findings, are instituting zero tolerance policies to end such verbal abuse.

Does emphasizing the power of language to influence our thoughts, perceptions, and behavior mean nonverbal communication is comparatively insignificant? It doesn't. It would be a major mistake to replace one communication myth with yet another one. Verbal and nonverbal communication typically act in tandem. Verbal abuse just discussed has a nonverbal component. The intensity of the abuse resides not just in the hurtful words but also in the tone of voice, facial expressions, gestures, and posture. Nonverbal communication is central to emotional expression, impression management, and much of what facilitates healthy relationships. For example, anxiety is chiefly communicated nonverbally. A smile can communicate a host of differing messages (e.g., approval, affection, sarcasm, contempt, discomfort). Eye contact is especially important to social connection.[22] The rise of multitasking on smartphones and other electronic devices is reducing eye contact. Note how often individuals don't even look up from their smartphones or laptops when conversing with someone standing in front of them. Social connection is illusory when we are distracted. Space and power are intricately connected. Those with the greatest power command the biggest space. The powerful may violate the space of the less powerful, but not vice versa. You can also determine nonverbally the socioeconomic status of individuals by observing people's level of *dis*connection when you speak to them.[23] Those born into privilege may exhibit disengagement by fidgeting, yawning, doodling, playing with social media, or otherwise showing disinterest. Mundane conversation may be viewed as "beneath them." Those of less fortunate means may feel more compelled to make a strong first impression, and so they remain attentive even if brain-killingly bored with the conversation.

Sometimes, however, verbal and nonverbal communication can occur together but produce mixed messages. A *mixed message* occurs when there is positive verbal and negative nonverbal communication, or vice versa. A "Customer Rage Study" revealed that the single most annoying catchphrase when respondents called to complain about a company's service was "Your call is important to us; please continue to hold."[24] The mixed message is the verbal expression of supposedly sincere concern for quality customer service but the nonverbal contradiction when complaining customers are forced to wait what can seem like a lifetime before talking to a customer service representative, assuming one ever answers.

What is apparent from this brief review is that *trying to quantify the importance of either verbal or nonverbal communication generally is simplistic*. Sometimes verbal communication becomes a focal point and of primary significance; other times nonverbal communication takes center stage. An example of verbal communication mounting center stage and assuming paramount attention is the interminable verbal scrum that emerged in vehement political posturing regarding the term *woke*. The word itself became the centerpiece of some political campaigns and dominated much political discourse leading to the 2024 national election. In March 2023, a *USA Today / Ipsos* national poll found the country split on the term, with 56% of respondents viewing it positively but 39% seeing it as a negative term.[25]

A classic example of nonverbal communication becoming the primary focus occurred during the 2015 Academy Awards show that actually began with reference to a verbal gaffe. Actor John Travolta at the 2014 Oscars inexplicably introduced Idina Menzel, the "Let It Go" singer from the movie *Frozen*, as Adele Dazeem. In an attempt to downplay the famous flub, Travolta and Menzel were chosen to present an Oscar at the 2015 Academy Awards. Host Neil Patrick Harris introduced the awkward pair to the audience with this quip: "Benedict Cumberbatch: It's not only the most awesome name in show business; it's also the sound you get when you ask John Travolta to pronounce 'Ben Affleck.'"[26] Before presenting the Oscar, Menzel referred to Travolta as her "very dear friend, Glom Gazingo." What had been to this point a slightly amusing recall of Travolta's embarrassing verbal goof became a compounding nonverbal mess that once again spotlighted Travolta's inept communication. Travolta grabbed Menzel's chin while flashing a broad smile (reportedly a mutually agreed-upon stunt). There was mild audience laughter at the somewhat uncomfortable attempt to be amusing, but then Travolta seemed incapable of letting go of Menzel's chin. He commenced to paw her face for what seemed to be the time it takes to gestate a baby. The Internet and social media exploded with comments about Travolta's "creepy face touching." Touching a person's face displays intimacy. It is normally off-limits for a stranger or an acquaintance.

The importance of nonverbal communication varies widely depending on several variables. As psychologist Jeff Thompson explains, one must consider the three Cs of nonverbal communication: context, clusters, and congruence.[27] Consider intercultural *context*. For example, pointing with your index finger is viewed as impolite in many cultures. In Brazil, the A-OK sign formed by making a circle with the thumb and index finger is equivalent to giving the middle finger in the United States. Americans often raise their index finger to signify "We're number one," but in Italy it means "We're number two," a less satisfactory source of celebratory pride. In the United States, nodding your head up and down communicates agreement and shaking it from side to side communicates disagreement. In Bulgaria, Turkey, and Iran, however, it is the opposite. In Greece, tipping the head back suddenly means "no," but in India it means "yes."[28] (Nod your head if you understand all of this.)

Clusters of nonverbal cues refer to avoiding the trap of giving too much importance to a single gesture apart from a constellation of different nonverbal cues. The oft-stated view that crossing your arms across your chest communicates defensiveness may be true, but if your shoulders are raised and your teeth are chattering and making the sound that emulates a woodpecker's rat-a-tat-tat on a tree trunk, then you just may be very cold.

Congruency refers to the agreement between verbal and nonverbal communication. A friend trips and flops onto a sidewalk. You quickly run to their aid and inquire about whether they are hurt. Your friend responds, "I'm fine, just klutzy," but you clearly see a grimace as if in pain, scratch marks on the face, and a quavering voice. This shows incongruency. The nonverbal (and vocal) cues signal discrepancy. In such cases, the nonverbal communication likely assumes correct meaning.

There is no specific number that indicates the importance of verbal or nonverbal communication generally. What may begin as a nonverbal incident could evolve into an animated verbal joust. So which is most important and by how much? There is no mathematical formula for such determinations, but those who confidently espouse precise numerical significance to verbal or nonverbal communication promulgate a myth.

Part II

BETWEEN YOU AND ME

9

MYTH: STOP STEREOTYPING

A *stereotype* is a fixed generalization about members of a group or social category. Stereotypes assign characteristics individuals have in common based on group categories that include gender identity, age, ethnic origin, socioeconomic status, religious affiliation, and even body type. For example, there is the American stereotype of older people being rigid in their thinking and experiencing physical and mental decline.[1] Stereotypes of Asian Americans as intelligent but nerdy, bad drivers, and unemotional are commonplace among non–Asian Americans.[2] This paints a picture of stereotypes as uniformly negative and inaccurate characterizations of groups. Psychologist Noam Shpancer describes what he considers to be this common misperception about all stereotypes: "There appears to be a broad consensus, among laypersons, and social scientists alike, that stereotypes . . . are patently lazy and distorted constructions, wrong to have and wrong to use."[3] Shpancer strongly rejects this common myth.

Stereotypes are not uniformly negative. *Some are positive* ("Artists are creative people"; "Nurses are empathic caregivers"). Stereotypes not only can be positive but they also can be *mostly accurate depictions when applied to some groups*. Notice that I didn't say "entirely accurate" because they are generalizations that will assuredly have individual exceptions. An example of a positive and mostly accurate stereotype is "College professors are highly educated and intelligent."[4] It would be depressing if this were not generally true. Another example is "Native Americans are spiritual and connected to nature." Professor Dale Nance of Case Western University counters the common misconception that all stereotypes are negative and inaccurate generalizations and should somehow be avoided: "It's naïve to say you can't use a generalization about a class of people unless it's universally valid—we use such stereotypes all the time and would be paralyzed without them."[5]

Stereotyping *permits rapid judgments when instant decisions are required* ("Is this a Good Samaritan or a dangerous person?"). You accidently stumble into an alley in a big city and you see three muscular young men covered in tattoos leaning against a building. Do you stereotype them as malevolent opportunists who would enjoy inflicting bodily harm and stealing your money, or do you allow for individual differences and take the chance that they are harmless, even angelic human beings by walking past them? As psychologist Noam Shpancer explains, "The ability to stereotype is often essential for efficient decision-making, which facilitates survival."[6] You don't ask a young child for parenting advice, and you don't ask a very old person to help you lift a very heavy object and carry it up a steep hill because you rely on stereotypes to make such decisions. You don't have to engage in careful contemplation: "Do I ask my six-year-old whether letting him watch violent videos is a good idea?"

Although stereotyping is usually applied to human behavior, we also have stereotypes of animals—assigning traits and attributes to specific animal species that influence us.[7] My experience with dogs, for example, has not always been positive. When I encounter a pit bull, even if it is being restrained by its owner, I always give it a wide berth for fear it may attack me. It is my "survival mechanism." I stereotype pit bulls as dangerous. Despite my friend Terry's animated assurance that his pit bull named Toby was "perfectly harmless," I always remained apprehensive and at a safe distance, including the day that both Terry and his wife Nancy had to grab Toby's collar and, with great difficulty, drag the snarling beast into their bedroom and lock him away as he clearly sought to eat me. Had I allowed for "individual differences" in this instance and not acted on my stereotype by maintaining a considerable distance from the dog, I would have been Toby's lunch. Are all pit bulls dangerous? No, but initially making a risk assessment and showing caution is reasonable. Once you get to know a particular dog who shows no aggressive tendencies and exhibits a warm, affectionate personality, you may realize that the stereotype in this instance does not apply. You can consciously overrule the stereotype, although in the case of pit bulls I am still wary regardless.

Despite the positive aspects of stereotyping as a built-in survival mechanism, *stereotypes can distort your perceptions and produce serious harmful consequences in some instances*.[8] Even positive stereotypes such as "women are nurturing and patient" may consign them, based on their gender, largely to supportive roles instead of leadership roles in groups and organizations.[9] One study used a video game simulation to determine whether stereotypes of African American men as "violent" would produce dangerous errors from participants who had to make quick decisions whether to fire at armed targets or to withhold fire when targets were unarmed. When the targets were African Americans, both Black and White participants made a significant number of errors, but far fewer when the targets were White. So mere knowledge of the stereotype may be enough to trigger erroneous deadly force.[10] This might explain the all-too-common instances where police officers, both Black and White, have shot unarmed African American men.[11]

Stereotyping can also create a *self-fulfilling prophecy*—acting on an originally false expectation that subsequently produces the expected belief or behavior to come true. Hundreds of studies show the power of self-fulfilling prophecies.[12] They can make stereotypes appear valid to the detriment of individuals who do not fit the generalization.[13] For example, if members of a team expect Asian students to be very quiet in group discussions (stereotype), they may ignore any Asian student when they attempt to contribute. Being ignored, they may give up trying to be heard by the group, thus "confirming" the expectation, though this particular student may not typically be quiet in groups (individual difference). Those individuals who most expect to be negatively stereotyped tend to avoid opportunities that could be corrective.[14]

Avoiding stereotyping is not the answer to its potential harmful effects because it can't be done. *Stereotyping is natural and unavoidable. It is a myth to think otherwise.* MRI-based brain studies reveal that stereotypes are activated in 170 milliseconds. That's not even a quarter of a second.[15] Suggesting that you "stop stereotyping" is useless advice, right up there with advising someone to "stop thinking."

There are communication strategies, however, that can constructively address stereotypes that should require ameliorative action.

1. *Confront the stereotypes directly.* Don't be shy about insisting on fair treatment and allowing for individual differences instead of broad generalizations about all members of a group. Such appeals can significantly reduce the effects of negative stereotyping and prejudiced attitudes.[16]

2. *Encourage contact.* Increasing contact with members of stereotyped groups can reduce negative stereotyping.[17] Perception is an inherently subjective human communication process. *There is no "immaculate perception."* Until we get to know other individuals, we may mistakenly lump them into a negative stereotype that is inaccurate. An analysis of 515 studies involving almost 250,000 participants supports the general wisdom of increasing contact with members of negatively stereotyped groups. Prejudice was reduced in 94% of the cases.[18] "Empathy with the out-group and a reduction in intergroup threat and anxiety" seem to be the "underlying mechanism of the phenomenon."[19] Positive contact works best under certain conditions, however: (1) contacts should be substantial not just superficial, (2) status differences among group members should be de-emphasized, (3) contact among relative equals (e.g., skill and education levels) works best, and (4) groups that pursue a common, valued goal can minimize negative stereotyping, even obliterate it eventually. A *superordinate goal*—one that requires mutual effort by everyone to achieve a desired end, such as a basketball team with substantial ethnic diversity striving for a championship—is most productive.[20] You can change a negative stereotype over time to a positive perception by reinforcing consistent positive experiences that can reset the instantaneous initial perception.

3. *Institute policies that disrupt negative stereotypes.* The implicit bias from negative stereotypes that men make better leaders than women, for example, can be mitigated by organizational policies that encourage diversity and hiring applicants from a broad range of gender identities and ethnicities. Training to overcome our negative habits of mind that identify negative stereotypes and provide activities that engender empathy for disadvantaged groups can also disrupt acting in accordance with negative stereotypes.[21]

Initially, stereotyping is automatic and unavoidable, but it matters how we act on potentially harmful stereotypes. Be open to individual differences, especially when careful risk assessments indicate potential positive outcomes, but recognize that such a risk assessment may prove protective when a negative stereotype is mostly accurate and caution may be prudent.

⑩

MYTH: SO MUCH OF VERBAL AND NONVERBAL COMMUNICATION IS JUST MEANINGLESS NOISE

Your partner asks when you arrive home from work, "How was your day?" What might be the effect if you answered, "Same old, same old," then walked away? Was curiosity about your partner's day really the salient point of the question, or were they just looking for connection? You're having lunch with a friend at a local restaurant. You attempt several times to start a conversation, but invariably, they check their text messages and make email responses while you both eat. Are you bothered by this? You offer assessments on the upcoming national elections in the company break room, but your coworker appears completely indifferent, even irritated. Are you discouraged from further interactions with this person?

There is a strong tendency to view much of what occurs during conversations or attempts to converse as meaningless noise, a distraction having no significance but provoking disinterest, even annoyance. Just reaching out to your partner nonverbally with a hug, peck on the cheek, or hand-holding can be mentally critiqued as "too needy." *This view that so much of what transpires verbally and nonverbally during interpersonal transactions is superficial and unimportant is mostly a myth.* Some conversations assuredly can be frivolous, tedious experiences devoid of wisdom and insight, but sometimes we just need to talk about the weather and not some deep philosophical discourse on the meaning of life or the sociological implications of why keyboard waffle irons exist. Even a simple greeting, "although it might seem trivial . . . begins the process of connection and starts conversations on the right foot."[1] Greetings are considered significant "across virtually all cultures and workplace contexts."[2] Research on these seemingly trivial transactions conducted by psychologist John Gottman and members of the Gottman Institute reveals: "These interactions may seem insignificant, but how you respond to them has a profound impact on the future of your relationships."[3] One study reported that daily conversation regardless of topic, just the act of talking to another person, helps maintain friendships and connection to others, but when such conversation, even about cat videos, decreases, it jeopardizes relationships.[4] Of course, if you never discuss much beyond Instagram photos or your latest health issues, this can be disconnecting just from redundancy and the boredom that ensues. Also, some nonverbal gestures of affection can be poorly timed and awkward, even unwanted, but reaching out to others is important when done appropriately.

These exchanges mistakenly deemed pointless, however, involve what Gottman terms *bids for connection*. A *connecting bid* is any attempt to engage another person in a positive transaction. Gottman explains that bids are "the fundamental unit of emotional communication."[5] There are verbal bids such as questions, statements, or comments whose content include thoughts, feelings, observations, opinions, or invitations. There are also nonverbal bids that are manifested by a facial expression, touch, gesture, or vocalization (e.g., "mm-hmm").

Connecting bids may be highly significant: "I love you" or "Do you want us to buy a house?" There are also seemingly trivial requests characteristic of daily communication: "Did you like dinner?" or "Did you read the email I sent to you?" Some are subtle attempts to connect: "Good morning," or "How was your trip?" Others can be very direct: "Are we still friends?" or "May I have your phone number?" A vague bid may protect our vulnerable self-esteem, whereas a direct bid may be too risky. For example, instead of asking directly "Do you want to go out to lunch with me tomorrow?" you might ask, "What's your favorite restaurant?" followed by "Maybe sometime we could have lunch there." The vague bid doesn't likely risk outright rejection as a more direct bid might because it doesn't put the person on the spot to answer unequivocally.

We all make connecting bids daily because we want to feel a part of the human experience, not separate and alone. We also want to connect in a meaningful way with the most significant people in our lives. Connecting bids, of course, don't always require an affirming response. A positive response to a connecting bid from an annoying individual harassing you for a date only encourages unwanted behavior. Nevertheless, *making bids and how you respond to the bids from others markedly influence the communication climate for relationships to blossom or wilt.*

Connecting bids will evoke three possible responses: turning toward, turning away, or turning against the bids.[6] A positive reaction to a connecting bid is called a *turning-toward response*. Your coworker tells an amusing story, and you laugh. A friend asks for help loading a truck, and you agree without complaint. A stranger on a bus wants to talk, and you engage in conversation. A parent invites you to breakfast, and you accept.

The *turning-away response* is an indifferent response to a bid. The recipient ignores a bid or acts preoccupied when a bid is made. You ask your partner if he wants his wash folded and put away, and he waves dismissively while preoccupied cruising social media. You ask a coworker for help on an important project, and without even glancing at you while reading a report, she mumbles, "Too busy." Turning-away responses communicate disinterest, a can't-be-bothered message to the bidder.

The *turning-against response* is an unambiguously negative rejection of a connecting bid. You ask your partner, "Do you want to watch some TV with me?" and your partner responds, "I'd rather eat broken glass. Try reading a book!" You offer to help your roommate clean up the clutter in your dorm room. Your roommate remarks, "Hey, Miss tidy bowl, learn to embrace the mess." You ask a coworker for assistance figuring out a new software program. The coworker responds, "I don't have a box of crayons to draw you a picture." The turning-against response is abrasive, even malicious.

Although turning-against responses may seem to be far more damaging to relationships than turning-away responses, research shows that *both are equally destructive*.[7] In fact, attempts to *rebid*—to try again after an initial bid has been ignored or rejected—are *near zero*. No one can or should be expected to turn toward every connecting bid, but a pattern of turning away or turning against connecting bids can destroy relationships.[8]

Most of those seemingly inconsequential, tedious verbal and nonverbal bids are the stuff of meaningful connections between people. Believing otherwise nurtures a communication myth. Making frequent bids and responding positively to those initiated by others cements relationships. Rarely initiating bids and responding negatively or indifferently to most bids damages relationships, and that damage may become irreparable. Research at the Gottman Institute reveals that *relationship masters* are those who "turned towards each other 86% of the time." *Relationship disasters* are those who "turned towards each other only 33% of the time."[9] What may appear to be meaningless can be the breath of life in a relationship.

MYTH: NEGATIVE-POSITIVE COMMUNICATION BALANCE SHOULD BE THE GOAL

If a new coworker were described to you as "vivacious, smart, friendly, and deceitful," what would be your impression of this person? Would the single negative characteristic neutralize the very positive descriptors? Conversely, if the same coworker were described to you as "crude, aggressive, unkind, and intelligent," would the single positive characteristic even make a dent in the negative first impression created by the initial negative qualities? Would you want to work with this person or cultivate a friendship?

If your reaction is as expected, then you are experiencing the *negativity bias*—the strong human tendency to be more strongly influenced by negative than by positive information. A single negative characteristic can override several positive qualities, but one positive attribute is unlikely to override several negative descriptors. Our brains respond more readily to negative information and events than to positive stimuli.[1] Your brain "is like Velcro for negative experiences but Teflon for positive ones."[2] Your amygdala, "the alarm bell of your brain," deploys about two thirds of its neurons to scour our environment for bad news. Why? Because negative information has the potential to threaten our well-being, but positive information poses little likely risk to our survival.[3] Most negative information, however, is relatively innocuous. You may be repelled by a coworker who is abrasive and has personal hygiene issues, but it is hardly cause for concern about your safety. Nevertheless, your brain is not prepared to make quick, nuanced assessments. Hesitation when faced with danger could prove fatal. "Gosh, is this a friendly bear or . . .?"—DEAD! It is best to be constantly vigilant.

The negativity bias can be especially problematic during job interviews.[4] Negative information can torpedo a candidate's chances. In a hypercompetitive job market, one clumsy remark during an interview may negate a very positive overall résumé.

Sometimes the negative information, however, should outweigh the positive. We don't absolve individuals when they commit a serious felony, even if it is their first ever and they have lived a spotlessly crime-free, even admirable life up to that point. If found guilty, they serve a prison sentence regardless. The one outweighs the many in this instance.

So, do we just balance negative communication with about equal amounts of positive communication to overcome the negativity bias? No! *That's the myth of balance.* In a *Forbes* article titled "Balancing Criticism and Praise," by a self-described "expert panel" of 13 associates of the Forbes Coaches Council, advice is offered on "how company leaders can balance necessary critique with praise for good work." They assert that "skewing too much to one side of this equation [criticism-praise] can leave employees confused by their leader's overly positive or negative focus and unable to improve their performance in meaningful ways."[5]

This striving for balance may seem to be a reasonable and effective strategy, but it ignores the negativity bias. Psychologist Richard Boyatzis at Case Western Reserve University explains, "You need the negative focus to survive, but a positive one to thrive. You need both, but in the right ratio."[6] Abundant research directly counters this mythical view that balance should be our goal. One study discovered that the highest-performing work teams made about *six times* as many positive comments ("Good point"; "Well done") as negative ones ("I disagree"; "That won't work") during members' transactions. In contrast, *the poorest-performing teams, on average, had a 3:1 negative-to-positive comments ratio.*[7] An abundance of positive information is usually required to overcome the negativity bias generally.[8] An analysis of almost 300 scientific studies that included more than 275,000 subjects validated the power of positivity.[9] What this research shows is that frequent positive communication, often called *supportive communication*, both verbally ("Good job"; "That's an interesting idea") and nonverbally (recognizing a coworker's birthday; sharing a meal with a coworker) can create a climate for success exhibited by satisfaction at work, increased salaries, and bolstered productivity, among other benefits.

Must you be unalterably positive to reap these benefits? That would be impractical, and probably rather annoying. Psychologist Barbara Fredrickson explains: "To experience 100-percent positivity defies and denies the humanness of life."[10] Studying voluminous data, however, she concluded that there is a "tipping point" that occurs when there is *at least a **3:1** positive-to-negative ratio in how we communicate with others, not episodically but globally over time.*[11] The ratio is a *pattern* not a single event. The Gottman Institute reports an even higher *"magic ratio" of 5:1* positive-to-negative interactions derived from studying thousands of couples in its "love lab."[12] For optimum results, the ratio is an even markedly higher *20:1* positive-to-negative interactions.[13] Recognize that the ratio is not 5:0 or 20:0. Even if your life is a bed of roses, there are thorns that are bound to prick your personal positivity even in the best of circumstances.

A key element of establishing a positive communication climate is avoiding defensive communication patterns. *Defensiveness* is a protective reaction to a perceived attack on one's self-concept and self-esteem. Defensive communication patterns increase negativity. There are several forms of defensive communication, but criticism, superiority, and incivility are at the top of the list.

Criticism can be deeply disturbing, especially when it is harsh and unexpected, but one study found that even mild criticism ("Make your emails less flowery or soft") can wound one's pride.[14] Another study found the disturbing result that high-achieving women in the workplace received *30 times more criticism on performance reviews than high-achieving men for the same behaviors*. There were no differences that could be attributed to whether the performance reviews were conducted by men or women.[15]

Criticism triggers a defensive reaction for two reasons: (1) it requires admitting mistakes if you accept the criticism as warranted, and (2) it devalues the recipient of the criticism.[16] Usual protective reactions to criticism include rejecting the validity of the criticism, counterattacking (the best defense is to go on the offense), or withdrawing.

Despite the potential damaging effects of criticism, a criticism-free life is a fantasy. As Aristotle observed, "There is only one way to avoid criticism: do nothing, say nothing, and be nothing." Criticism is warranted if individuals or groups are underachieving, acting disruptively, or imperiling oneself and others by making dangerous choices. Criticism, however, does not have to be caustic and hurtful. How you deliver the message is essential.[17] Here are some examples:

1. *Suggest with descriptive I-statements.* An *I-statement* seems less like an attack and more like a description of changes that need to be made than a *You-statement.* Consider the difference in these two statements: "You've made some mistakes on this report" versus "I think this is a solid report, but I have just a few suggestions." The I-statement avoids pointing the finger of blame and offers to help, not diminish the person.[18] Any statement that starts with "You haven't . . ." or "You didn't . . ." or a similar phrase signals an accusation and can instantly ignite defensiveness.

2. *Describe behaviors, not perceived character defects.* Statements such as "You're weak" or "You're uncaring" identify perceived character flaws. Constructive feedback describes what behavioral change is desired. "I'm frustrated when dinner is delayed. Could we work together on prepping for meals the night before so that dinner is ready earlier?" seeks a specific behavior that can potentially fix the problem collaboratively.

3. *Give praise.* Praise is highly valued but often missing.[19] Understand, however, that praising inauthentically or indiscriminately may be counterproductive. It dilutes the sincerity and positive impact it can have on recipients. You don't want to create a perception that you are phony or manipulative. Consequently, praise should not be a daily checklist: "Complimented my partner—check!" Also, don't praise mundane behavior that should be taken for granted, such as: "Well done! You showed up to work on time";

"Way to put the toilet seat down." Praise meaningful accomplishments. Here are some quick steps for praising effectively:

a) *Praise should be specific not vague.* "You handled that customer complaint very skillfully by keeping calm and constructive" is preferable to "You are a good worker." Vague praise offers no direction for what particular behavior should be repeated.

b) *Praise effort that can lead to meaningful accomplishments.* Even if effort fails to achieve desired results, praising effort can motivate trying again, not giving up. "You made the effort and that counts even though it didn't work out this time. Don't be discouraged. Keep trying."

c) *Praise improvement.* Waiting until a desired outcome has been achieved ignores the role praise can play as a motivator for improvement. This is particularly important when couples are trying to repair their faltering relationships. Improvement that falls short of goal achievement still deserves praise.

The relationship between criticism and praise has been debated with a *criticism sandwich*—praise-criticize-praise—offered as a preferred way of delivering negative feedback. Psychologist Clifford Nass, however, disputes this advice, arguing that the human brain forgets the praise (positive feedback) when the more impactful criticism (negative feedback) ensues.[20] Individuals tend to expect a "but" immediately following initial praise, signaling that criticism will follow. Nass suggests instead starting with criticism, then following that with plentiful praise. I have ambivalent feelings about both approaches. My preference is that meaningful praise be offered in other contexts separate from criticism. The more opportunities, where we can "but out" and just offer praise without a negative qualifier to follow, the better. Yes, praise can reduce the sting of criticism, and that is useful, but when praise regularly gets partnered with criticism, the praise can easily disappear from our consciousness because of the negativity bias.

Superiority, a second defensive communication pattern, communicates the message that one is me-deep in self-importance. Superiority, or arrogance as it is often termed, can alienate most people. It blatantly says, "I'm better than you." Whatever the differences in our abilities, talents, and intellect, treating people as equals on a human level is constructive. This does not mean we all have the same abilities. It means that, regardless of status or hierarchical titles, you give each person an equal opportunity to succeed and exhibit whatever potential they possess, and to share their wisdom where appropriate. Everyone has flaws. In fact, one way of minimizing defensiveness is to share your own shortcomings with others.[21] A national study found that 91% of employees reported that their job satisfaction increased significantly when managers admitted mistakes.[22] Self-deprecating humor that makes fun of oneself can also be an effective means of reducing the spotlight on status differences and diminishing potential defensiveness that can attend power-difference dynamics.[23] Here's an example from a study on using humor: "So, last night, my partner gave me some good advice about this presentation. She said, 'Whatever you do don't try to be too charming, witty, or intellectual . . . just be yourself!'"[24] When a person pokes fun at themselves it just makes them seem more human, approachable. It is the opposite of egotism. If you do it too often, however, or from a position of low status, it can produce perceptions of weak confidence and a slim skill set. Appropriateness has to be considered.

Finally, *incivility*, a third defensive communication pattern, consists of acts of rudeness and disrespect communicated both verbally and nonverbally. A poll conducted by Christine Porath, author of *Mastering Civility: A Manifesto for the Workplace*, found that 80% of respondents admitted losing time on their job ruminating about even mild instances of disrespect, while 78% were less committed to their employer, and half decreased their effort because of workplace incivility.[25] Name-calling and vulgarity are typically viewed as the most blatant and unacceptable forms of incivility.

Civility treats people with respect. As Porath explains, "Civility is smart, it's savvy, it's human. By being civil, you get to be a nice person, and you get ahead. People are more likely to support you and work harder for you."[26] Even brief exposure to civil discourse can enhance a positive communication climate across a broad range of contexts.[27] Remaining unconditionally civil and encouraging others to do likewise can alter the tone and improve the potential for constructive outcomes of disputes.

In summary, remember that the "magic ratio" is not 1:1 positive to negative. You're not striving for an equitable balance between the two. That promotes a communication myth. The communication pattern to overcome the negativity bias requires a sizable imbalance of much more positive than negative communication for the best outcomes to occur. This requires supportive instead of defensive communication patterns.

⓬

MYTH: POWER IS RELATIONSHIP POISON

Lord Acton, an English historian, purportedly asserted, "Power tends to corrupt, and absolute power corrupts absolutely." This is a popular perspective except perhaps among those who wield power. As former Secretary of the Navy John Lehman once quipped, "Power corrupts. Absolute power is kind of neat." Viewing power as coercive and a negative communication force is reflected in common phrases such as "power struggles," "power plays," "power grabs," "abuses of power," and "power politics." Research on the communication behavior of high-power individuals doesn't engender a warm, fuzzy counterpoint to this depiction. As social psychologist Dacher Keltner disturbingly concludes based on his decades of study, there is a "wealth of evidence that having power makes people more likely to act like sociopaths."[1] He notes that high-power individuals are prone to unethical behavior such as humiliating less powerful individuals, lying, repeated abusive behavior toward others, and a troubling lack of empathy.[2]

Power, however, can be used for good or ill purposes. Some may use power to exploit vulnerable individuals for personal gain at the expense of individual and group goal attainment. Others may use power productively to achieve professional and team goals, resolve interpersonal conflicts, and sustain important personal relationships.

Power can be a force for good, as exhibited by such powerful historical events as the civil rights movement, the struggle to address climate change, and marriage equality, to provide a mere sample. *It is just a myth to assume that power is inevitably a negative force in relationships*. There is nothing laudable about exercising little power.[3] Weakness relative to others can strain interpersonal relationships, trigger stress, promote apathy and diminish motivation, erode individuals' self-esteem, and ignite destructive interpersonal and group conflict.[4] Power is intrinsically embedded in all relationships. Keltner concludes that "intensive studies from around the world have found that power is part of every relationship. . . all relationships prove to be defined by mutual influence."[5] Your choice is not between using or not using power. "We only have options about whether to use power destructively or productively for ourselves and relationships."[6]

So, defining power and its three types can determine when it is destructive and when it is productive. *Power* is the ability to influence the attainment of goals sought by you or others. "Power is never the property of an individual; it belongs to a group and remains in existence only so long as the group keeps together."[7] For example, a person can be viewed as a powerful leader at work capable of extraordinary achievements, but viewed as an inept disaster at home with their family, branded as hopelessly ineffectual, especially by teenage children. So, is this person powerful or powerless? *No one is completely powerless*, although they may feel that way at times.

"Powerful or powerless" is a *false dichotomy*—an either-or choice between two options when at minimum a third option is possible. Power is a matter of degree, not an either-or choice. Ever see a child pitch a fit in a grocery store, demanding some sweet in a high-decibel voice, and see the parents capitulate to the demand just to make the obnoxious din cease for the benefit of everyone? Who's in charge in this little drama, the parents or the child? If each person has some degree of power in any relationship, then the germane question is not "Who is powerful and who is powerless?" The relevant question is "How much power does one person have compared to another person?"

There are three forms of power, and they are considerably different from each other.[8] *Dominance* is the *active* exercise of *power over* others. Power struggles often ensue from exercising dominance. For example, there is this story of a captain who spots a light in the distance, exactly in the path of his ship. He gives an order that the following message be sent: "Turn 10 degrees south." He receives this response: "*You* need to turn 10 degrees north." Annoyed that his order has been ignored and he has been told to change course, the captain orders a second message be transmitted: "I am this ship's captain, and I order you to turn 10 degrees south." The captain receives an immediate reply: "I am a seaman second class, and I am telling you to turn 10 degrees north." The captain is now outraged that a lowly seaman second class is thumbing his nose in blatant disregard of the chain of command. The captain in a near fury responds: "This is a battleship coming right at you; turn 10 degrees south." This prompts an instant reply: "This is a lighthouse; turn 10 degrees north." The captain expects absolute obedience because of his rank. He assumes that his legitimate entitlement to strict obedience should be unquestioned. Persistent fighting about who should be dominant in this contentious transaction, however, could have ended up with a battleship on top of a lighthouse.

Dominance has consequential implications. Bosses can interrupt an employee project team without asking permission to bloviate about the wonders of rule changes in major league baseball, but team members may feel obligated to endure the irrelevant rant in somnolent silence or ingratiating agreement. More consequentially, sexual harassment is fundamentally an abuse of the dominance form of power. Quid pro quo harassment (something for something) occurs when the more powerful person requires sexual favors from the less powerful person in exchange for landing an employment promotion or job perks, or avoiding being fired or demoted. Close to half of the women who have been sexually harassed at work leave their jobs, even switch careers.[9] This diminishes their chain of experience to compete for top-level positions.

Workplace bullying is also fundamentally rooted in a dominance form of power. Workplace bullying is pervasive.[10] Bullying persists primarily because most transgressors (legitimate authorities) are in more powerful positions than victims. Toxic bosses create significant group and organizational harm.[11] Their rage and abuse is typically a cover for their own deficiencies as leaders.[12] Coworker bullying is less frequent but can occur especially in the case of LGBTQ+ workers because of ugly prejudice. Coworkers may seem to be equal in power, but bullying the more reticent or vulnerable individuals is still an example of dominance. Higher-ups who could address the problem constructively often ignore bullying.

Prevention is a *reactive* form of power used to impede or take *power from* those with greater influence. Those who attempt to dominate others are often faced with either defiance or resistance from the dominator's targets. *Defiance* is unambiguous, purposeful noncompliance. Those in authority are anxious to halt defiance because it can be contagious, especially with ready access to social media enabling awareness and encouragement of such acts. Defiance should be a choice of last resort because defiant individuals can be socially ostracized or they can be severely punished. In the workplace, defiance of a supervisor's dictates can be labeled as "insubordination," then used as reason to demote or terminate a defiant employee.

Resistance is covert, ambiguous noncompliance in the face of perceived dominance by others. Adept resistance can leave everyone wondering if it even happened. Resistance strategies are often referred to as passive aggression.[13] The passive part is a willingness on the surface to obey the dominant individual's edicts. The aggressive part is acting under the surface to sabotage the dominant person's wishes by creating difficulties. Among a host of passive-aggressive strategies, there are the following: feigned ignorance about how to perform certain tasks that aren't that challenging; intentional sloppy, inept performance when required to attempt a task; deliberately misunderstanding instructions that might result in costly errors; and purposely procrastinating to prolong a task until, in utter frustration, the dominant person gives the job to a more "capable," less troublesome individual. The point of resistance is to make life difficult for those in powerful positions. Their actions say, "Yes, you can force compliance, but at what cost?" *Those who are defiant dig in their heels, but those who resist merely drag their feet.*

Although defiance is chosen in some instances, resistance is far more often the choice of the less powerful. Resistance has an advantage over defiance. It is often safer to use indirect means of noncompliance than direct confrontation. Outright defiance leaves no ambiguity about a person's intentions. Passive-aggressive strategies, however, can seem murky. Punishing someone for behavior that is not clear-cut noncompliance but possibly only insufficiently skillful can provoke backlash from others who might complain about injustice and unfairly harsh reactions. "Hey, I'm doing what you told me to do," says the resister, trying to camouflage intentions to resist. Yes, they do marginally comply, but slowly, methodically, and with minimum effectiveness to provoke maximum frustration from those with greater power. Isn't it just easier to pass the task to someone more compliant?

Defiance and resistance are matters of appropriateness. Defiance may be a moral imperative in certain circumstances in which unethical or dangerous behavior is mandated. Resistance may be the only way less powerful individuals can fight against injustice and poor treatment. Confronting either, however, can be a constructive step, especially when the defiance or resistance is unwarranted. (Confronting constructively is discussed extensively in the next chapter.) You don't want to enable bad behavior by acquiescing to unreasonable defiance or resistance. Sometimes, when dealing with a passive aggressor, you must thwart the enabling process by making sure consequences result from resistance. Allow for human failing, but when a pattern strongly suggests resistance strategies are being employed, require compensation for any damage resulting from passive aggression, or continue a meeting without waiting for a late arrival.

Empowerment is a *proactive* form of power derived from enhancing the capabilities, choices, and influence of individuals and groups. It is *power to* accomplish individual and group goals. It counters the myth of power as an inevitable negative force in relationships. Empowerment promotes power sharing and dissuades power struggles. The group profits from all members gaining the ability to succeed together. For example, group members who improve their speaking skills for a class presentation benefit the entire group.

Individuals become empowered by learning to communicate competently. Acquiring communication knowledge and developing a broad range of communication skills can give you the confidence to adapt your communication appropriately in a wide variety of communication situations. Assertiveness is one of these key communication skills that empowers. *Assertiveness* is "the ability to communicate the full range of your thoughts and emotions with confidence and skill."[14] The terms *assertive* and *aggressive* are not the same communication behavior despite frequent confusion about differences.[15] Those who confuse assertiveness with aggressiveness tend to ignore the "with confidence and skill" part of this definition. That's the communication competence part. Assertiveness isn't forcing your thoughts and emotions on others (inappropriateness). Too often bluster and bullying are excused as "simply being assertive." Assertiveness necessitates competent communication of thoughts and feelings, not some infantile, cathartic rant dressed up in a scary clown suit to frighten a person or group into submission.

Assertiveness falls between the extremes of aggressiveness and passivity. Aggressiveness puts one's own needs first; you wipe your shoes on other people. Passivity underemphasizes one's own needs; you're a doormat in a world of muddy shoes. Assertiveness embraces one's own needs but also the needs of others. You don't stomp on others, and you don't let others stomp on you.

Although assertiveness can be used to defy others, it is primarily an empowering skill, a positive exercise of power. Dacher Keltner, based on extensive research, concludes, "Your power expands as you empower others." Assertive individuals try to enhance their significance in the eyes of others, not alienate anyone. Keltner continues, "People gain power . . . by speaking up first, offering a possible answer to a problem, being first to assert an opinion, freeing up everyone's thinking by throwing out a wild suggestion, question, or humorous observation that gets the creative juices flowing."[16] When shy individuals learn assertiveness, they become more productive contributors. When aggressive individuals learn assertiveness, they can transform the relationship climate from negative to positive. Assertiveness requires practice, and it involves several steps.

1. *Describe behaviors that relate to your feelings.* Describe behaviors that tap into your feelings, such as, "I feel anxious (feeling) when we fail to meet our deadlines (behavior)." Recognize, however, that "I feel" is not an incantation, a phrase capable of magically achieving a desired goal. For example, "I feel that an infant suck-

ing on a pacifier is acting more maturely than you are" is obviously aggressive not assertive. Inflammatory language just ignites verbal flame wars so pervasive on the Internet, and pretending to soften verbal attacks with an "I feel" beginning tries to be aggressive hoping others will accept nastiness as assertive.

2. *Monitor your nonverbal cues.* Research reveals that the majority of people do not accurately perceive how they come across to other people: either passive, assertive, or aggressive.[17] Dozens of times I have conducted a very simple exercise to underline how challenging this can be. I form groups of 6–8 seated members. Each person in turn issues the simple statement, "Stand up." Participants individually obey and physically rise from their chairs when they perceive the statement to be assertive, not aggressive or passive. Those who remain seated provide feedback (e.g., "Too aggressive"; "That sounded like you're begging"). Each person remains standing until all group members have risen. Once everyone has stood up, sometimes sporadically and other times in unison, the statement is changed to "Sit down" with the same instructions. The statements "Stand up" and "Sit down" seem to be inherently aggressive commands, and raising one's voice can certainly enhance that perception. Yet each statement can be communicated passively through a complex nonverbal stew composed of hesitant or questioning upraised tone of voice, weak or absent eye contact, nervous and frozen facial expressions, and soft-spokenness that can sometimes come off as almost a whisper. This is a surprisingly challenging exercise for most people. I have witnessed innumerable individuals grow increasingly frustrated that other people perceive aggressiveness when they believe that they have toned down the statements to be assertive, even passive. It's especially interesting to watch CEOs of major corporations stumble over this simple exercise in apparent exasperation in front of their employees. This exercise underlines that too often we do not monitor our nonverbal communication. We are clueless regarding how we come across to others. Pay attention to how others react to the way you communicate messages. Seek feedback.

3. *Specify the behavior or objective you are seeking.* Aimless assertiveness won't accomplish much. Provide a target: "Perhaps we could meet Tuesdays and Thursdays for the next two weeks, if that works for everyone's schedule." Notice that this is not issued as an order but as a suggestion.

4. *Identify positive outcomes.* Emphasize positive not negative outcomes. Remember the negativity bias. "This presentation will be great when we get it together, so let's get busy organizing it." This is a better statement than "If we don't get our presentation organized we'll fail."

Those who harbor a negative concept of power are usually responding to dominance and its companion form—prevention. Although likely to remain prevalent in our competitive society, the dominance-prevention power struggle is a poor communication model and promotes the myth that power in relationships is detrimental. "Social science reveals that one's ability to get or maintain power, even in small group situations, depends on one's ability to understand and advance the goals of other group members."[18] Dominance-prevention cycles will not end, and such uses of power can be a negative force in relationships. Empowerment, however, can gain a wider audience and expand our appreciation for ways that power can be a positive communication force to enhance our relationships and achieve our desired goals.

⓭

MYTH: CONFLICT IS THE DEATH STAR OF RELATIONSHIPS

"**W**e never argue." Sound familiar? The clear implication is that the strength and stability of our interpersonal relationships depend on keeping conflict at bay. This mythical belief that healthy relationships experience little if any conflict and, conversely, relationships in deep trouble are precariously balancing on the cliff of extinction because of fairly frequent conflict is quite common. Dr. John Gottman, based on more than 40 years of extensive research with thousands of couples, however, states, "Although we tend to equate a low level of conflict with happiness, a lasting relationship results from a couple's ability to manage the conflicts that are inevitable in any relationship."[1] In fact, research by the Gottman Institute reveals that "couples who do not fight at all are more likely to end up divorced."[2] They are usually avoiding underlying disagreements eating away at a harmonious relationship. Research reveals that conflict is a very common challenge, especially in groups, whether it occurs regarding group tasks, relationship tension, or process (decision-making) considerations.[3]

Conflict for most people is as welcome as a jilted lover at a wedding ceremony. Managing conflict effectively is uncommon, so the view that conflict seems destructive is not surprising.[4] *It's not the frequency of conflict, but how competently it is managed, that is of paramount importance.* Effectively managed conflict can instigate positive changes, promote creative problem-solving and innovative thinking, and encourage power balancing.[5] "The key to effective team negotiation and group decision making is constructive dissent—disagreements that respectfully and productively challenge others' viewpoints."[6]

Although conflict can be constructive, it can also be destructive when managed poorly. So, what distinguishes the two? *Destructive conflict* is exhibited and nurtured by communication that aims to dominate others, and easily escalates into acts of retaliation, hyper-competitiveness, defensiveness, and stubborn inflexibility.[7] Such conflict can easily spiral out of control as participants focus more on hurting an adversary than achieving an initial goal. When you begin to realize during a contentious engagement, "Gee, I'm getting stupid" because you are employing petty, infantile tactics to avoid losing an argument, you have entered the danger zone of destructive conflict.[8]

Consider this event as an illustration of destructive conflict. Dr. David Dao, a 69-year-old physician and passenger on United Airlines flight 3411, became the unfortunate individual randomly chosen by a computer to leave the plane against his will because the flight had been overbooked. Too few passengers volunteered to accept an offer of $800 and a free hotel stay, so Dao was the "winner" of the boot-you-off lottery. He insisted that leaving the flight meant that patients he needed to see the next morning would be disadvantaged and perhaps harmed. He would not be able to catch another flight until the next day, so he politely refused to leave the plane. Officers from the Chicago Department of Aviation came on board and aggressively dragged him from his seat, causing him to suffer a severe concussion, the loss of two front teeth, and a broken nose.

Another passenger video recorded the startling event and posted it on social media. The response was swift. One person posted, "United: You may be asked to vacate or be taken off the plane by force, but for $49.99 you can upgrade to trial by combat." Another person posted, "In the unlikely event of an overbooking, please assume the crash position whilst we hunt down volunteers." Yet another individual offered this sarcastic response, "United: Putting the hospital in hospitality." So, despite Dr. Dao's reasonable objection to being required to leave his flight, and observations from other passengers who later reported that he was "very polite" when asked to leave, officers called to enforce his removal made only a perfunctory attempt to resolve the disagreement peacefully. Upon his rejection of the minimal effort made by officers, and with stubborn inflexibility from airline employees who provided no alternative such as increasing the compensation to encourage anyone else to volunteer, suddenly the conflict was escalated by the officers, and Dr. Dao was treated as a criminal.[9]

Constructive conflict by contrast is exhibited and nurtured by communication that tries to de-escalate the conflict from flying out of control, and approaches the disagreement cooperatively with a focus on problem-solving, rather than "winning" in combat, everything not exhibited by those in authority during the Dao incident.[10] The emphasis is on trying to construct a viable solution that is mutually satisfactory to all parties in the conflict. Even if this fails, the communication process that typifies constructive conflict permits parties that disagree to maintain cordial relationships. Supportive not defensive communication patterns, as discussed in Chapter 11, are essential.

Keeping conflict constructive requires competent communication. Thus, research on communication styles of conflict management has been extensive. A *communication style of conflict management* is a particular pattern of communicating when trying to manage a conflict. The five such styles are the following: collaborating, accommodating, compromising, avoiding, and competing.[11]

Collaborating is the most complicated but usually the most beneficial. The *collaborating style* focuses on what Daniel Shapiro, founder and director of the Harvard International Negotiation Program, terms the "relentless We."[12] You never take your eye off what path can be taken to achieve mutually satisfactory outcomes for all parties to the conflict. This is a win-win style, not a win-lose competitive fight-to-the-death approach. *You balance both task (job to be accomplished) and social (relationships) considerations.*

Collaborating requires greater-than-ordinary communication skills. It has three primary components: confrontation, integration, and smoothing. Despite the common media use of confrontation to mean violent protest, *confrontation* here is defined as the overt recognition that conflict exists and the effort to manage conflict in a productive way for all parties.[13] Confrontation incorporates assertive and support-ive communication skills already addressed (see chapters 11 and 12). Some issues, however, do not benefit from confrontation. Trivial differences of opinion when confronted can be like irritating online pop-up ads. *Integration* attempts to devise creative solutions that satisfy all parties involved. For example, when standard budgetary sources are scarce and ignite conflict regarding how to divide a slim resource pie, crowdfunding to expand the resource pie with new money can reduce or even eliminate the conflict.[14] Finally, attempting to calm the agitated feelings of individual or group members when a conflict erupts is called *smoothing*. When tempers flare and anger morphs into screaming and shedding of tears, no collaboration is possible. "Let's all take a breather, then start fresh without attacking each other, OK?" is an example of smoothing.

The second communication style of conflict management called *accommodating* is also referred to as *yielding* to the concerns and desires of others. Accommodators show a high concern for social relationships but low concern for task accomplishment. Generally, the less powerful are expected to accommodate those with more power. Although most people view accommodating as appeasement, a group that has experienced protracted strife may welcome yielding even on an issue of minor importance.[15] From my own experience, as an example, my wife Marcy and I do not agree about making our bed each day. We initially clashed about her preference. Marcy prefers a made bed and I do not, except on rare occasions. I accommodate her preference, however, by sharing the task. Accommodation does not have to be viewed as total capitulation but instead as a loving act. I make the accommodation because I embrace the wisdom of the "magic ratio," the minimum 5:1 positive-to-negative communication that strengthens relationships, as discussed in Chapter 11. When Marcy goes on her annual 5-day retreat at a local retreat facility, however, I don't make the bed, but I do text her a photo of the unmade bed as a serial joke. This is not an example of compromising because Marcy gives up nothing. Likewise, her acquiescence of my seeming need to control the TV remote also is not a compromise, but a loving accommodation.

A third communication style of conflict management, *compromising*, requires giving up something to get something in return. Those who compromise show a moderate concern for both task and social relationships. Compromisers seek workable but not necessarily optimal solutions. We may not like to compromise, but something is better than nothing. When an integrative solution is unattainable, when a temporary agreement is the only practical option, or when the issues involved are not considered critical to the group or couple, compromise can be appropriate.

Avoiding is a communicating style of withdrawing from potentially disagreeable struggles. Flights from fights can seem constructive because they circumvent unpleasantness. Someone using the avoiding style, however, exhibits only minimal concern for both task and social relationships. Avoiders hope conflict will disappear if ignored. Instead, it may increase relationship conflict.[16] Could you just avoid your partner's substance abuse as it threatens to destroy your relationship?

Avoiding, however, may be appropriate in some instances.[17] Low-power individuals may avoid contentious issues with high-power persons as a kind of self-preservation. Confronting a boss, for example, who intensely dislikes being challenged may get you fired. Avoiding some persistent sources of disagreement may prove to be constructive. According to long-term studies by the Gottman Institute, *69% of all marital conflicts never go away*, and arguments keep recurring year after year.[18] These are called *serial arguments*. Get used to the idea that there is no "right way" to load toilet paper onto the holder—over or under? Surveys reveal that this is a surprisingly contentious issue.[19] You may decide that whoever loads the toilet roll gets to decide over or under, but avoid persistently resurrecting this niggling issue. You may need to live with one of life's little disappointments. Couples sometimes keep resurrecting points of contention, some petty and some very troublesome, and like someone picking a scab, they reopen old wounds repeatedly. Avoiding in such cases is usually wise. Aside from serial arguments, however, avoiding in most instances does not lead to competent conflict management.[20]

Addressing conflict as a win-lose contest is using another communication style called *competing/power-forcing*. Someone using this style exhibits a high concern for task but low concern for relationships. This style, sometimes referred to as *hard bargaining*, is communicated in a variety of ways that are likely to produce destructive conflict:

threats, criticism, contempt, abusive remarks and jokes, sarcasm, ridicule, intimidation, denials of responsibility, and firing employees.[21] Those using the competing/power-forcing style are being aggressive. They're trying to force compliance.

Power-forcing typically produces *psychological reactance*, a theory developed by Jack Brehm to explain why the more someone tries to control us by trying to force compliance the more we are inclined to resist such efforts or even to do the opposite.[22] This bit of whimsical wisdom captures the basis of psychological reactance: "There are three ways to make sure something gets done—do it yourself; hire someone to do it; *forbid* your kids to do it."

Competing/power-forcing strategies challenge our sense of personal freedom to choose.[23] The COVID-19 mask-wearing conflict illustrates this in a stark way.[24] Tell someone they can't do something (e.g., forbid shopping in a store unless wearing a mask) and often it is what many individuals want to do most. Consider a common scenario. Imagine while returning to your car in a congested parking lot that another car follows you and then waits for your space. Would you hasten your departure or slow it down deliberately? What if your parking stalker honks to encourage a faster exit? One study tested this exact scenario and discovered that most people slow their exit, especially if honked at.[25] When I posed this scenario to numerous classes, there was usually a divided result when the car is just waiting, but when the driver honks most students responded negatively, such as, "I'd browse my smartphone until the jerk left" and even more aggressive reactions usually involving the middle finger gesture. Such is the typical response to perceived power-forcing strategies.

Research clearly favors some conflict styles over others, even though more than one style may need to be used over the course of a conflict.[26] Overall, the collaborating style is the most constructive and produces the greatest satisfaction from all parties in conflict.[27] Avoiding typically produces poor results and can induce *groupthink*, a defective decision-making process that can culminate in disastrous group decisions.[28] Group members "go along to get along" even when decisions are thought to be potentially cataclysmic. Dissent is discouraged, even punished, and groupthink occurs. The power-forcing style is least effective.[29] It tends to promote destructive conflict.[30] You have a choice. As author Max Lucado observes, "Conflict is inevitable, but combat is optional."[31]

Despite the clear benefits of collaborating, poor results of avoiding, the disadvantages of power-forcing, and mixed results for accommodating and compromising, *we seem to use the least effective styles most often to manage conflict*.[32] Numerous workplace studies show the power-forcing style as the most common approach used by managers, both men and women, with employees.[33] The same is true when employees engage in conflict with their peers.[34]

Competing/power-forcing should be a style of last resort, used in emergencies, for example, when collaboration is too time consuming and avoiding could be counterproductive, even catastrophic in emergency situations. Addressing disruptive group members may ultimately require power-forcing when all else fails. In one study of disruptive group members, no matter how talented team members were, those groups that had to deal with a persistent "bad apple" who didn't respond constructively when confronted scored 30% to 40% lower on a challenging task than teams with no such person.[35] Analyzing data from 50,000 employees at 11 businesses, two researchers found that *the average benefit derived from firing a toxic employee is about four times greater than adding a good employee*. Even adding a superstar employee, someone in the top 1% of job performance, doesn't negate a toxic group member. *Dumping the toxic employee is twice as beneficial financially as hiring the superstar*.[36] Power-forcing does have its place in limited circumstances.

In summary, conflict is not inherently bad or necessarily an indicator of interpersonal relationships in trouble. Voluminous research shows that how we manage conflict is critical. Those communication styles of conflict management such as competing/power-forcing and avoidance are likely to produce destructive conflict that you don't want to increase in frequency. Communication styles such as collaborating and sometimes accommodation and compromise can produce constructive conflict that can be beneficial.

⓮

MYTH: TAME YOUR TEMPER BY VENTING YOUR ANGER

One of my favorite bumper stickers is "Wag more, bark less." I have never been awakened at night by a dog's wagging tail, but I certainly have been roused by incessant canine barking that can provoke my anger. The American Psychological Association notes, "Anger is a completely normal, usually healthy, human emotion. But when it gets out of control and turns destructive, it can lead to problems."[1] Anger is a very common emotional expression of dissatisfaction often poorly controlled. "The experience of anger in the workplace is ubiquitous—some estimates report that half of all employees feel 'a little angry at work,' with approximately one fourth of workers experiencing chronic anger in the workplace."[2] Anger is also common in romantic relationships, friendships, and familial relationships.[3] The most common communication behaviors associated with anger include yelling, swearing, flinging insults, crying, giving dirty looks, making angry gestures, throwing things, and physical assault. Then there's nasty, not necessarily apparent retaliatory anger, illustrated by an unattributed joke: "A husband says to his wife, 'When I get angry at you, you never fight back. How do you control your anger?' His wife replies, 'I clean the toilet.' 'How does that help?' inquires her husband. She answers, 'I use your toothbrush.'"

Learning to address anger effectively is an important step in managing conflicts competently, but as I will make apparent, it is a myth that venting our anger is an effective means of managing it.[4] Before addressing this common myth, let's first clearly draw distinctions between destructive and constructive anger to gain important perspective. *Three conditions determine how destructive or constructive anger is.*[5] The first condition is *frequency*, or how often anger occurs. An occasional anger event may be hardly noticed by romantic partners or coworkers. Angry outbursts on almost a daily basis, however, are cause for concern. A second condition is the *intensity*, or relative strength, of the anger. The intensity of one's anger can vary from inconsequential annoyance to out-of-control rage. Anger that is on the milder side can be constructive. It can create attention to an ignored problem, and it can be a first step toward discussing and implementing important change. Rage, however, can make a person look deranged. As humorist Will Rogers once remarked: "People who fly into a rage always make a bad landing." Temper tantrums and screaming fits can appear childish and undisciplined. In intimate relationships, rage scares partners and children. In the workplace, rage will likely get you fired, or if it is the boss who is enraged, the entire workplace climate is polluted.[6] Pets, neighbors, and innocent bystanders can also be affected. As Eleanor Roosevelt once noted: "Anger is one letter short of danger." *Duration*, or how long the anger lasts, is the third condition that identifies anger as either constructive or destructive. The length of an anger episode can vary from short-lived to prolonged. Quick flashes of temper may hardly cause a ripple of attention from others, especially when they are infrequent. Even fairly intense expressions of anger, if short-lived, can make the point powerfully that you are upset. Protracted anger episodes, however, can make conflict management extremely difficult and brand a person as volatile. When expressions of anger are frequent, highly intense, and long lasting, the combination can be extremely combustible.

There is a popular myth that venting one's anger is an effective means of managing it so it doesn't become destructive, while suppressing anger is thought to be counterproductive.[7] Recently, this myth has been popularized by what is dubbed a "rage ritual," a ceremony in which participants express their intense anger about some issue or event in their past by screaming and violently swinging and smashing sticks. This usually occurs in a wooded area and lasts for at least 20 minutes or until ragers are too pooped to raise their arms. Organized rage rituals are most popular with women and can cost between $2,000 to $4,000.[8]

Extensive research, however, reveals that *venting anger, or "blowing off steam," as in rage rituals, usually increases one's anger.*[9] It replays our anger in unhealthy explosions. This doesn't quell the anger. It awakens it, pops it out of bed, and starts it doing jumping jacks. Venting can easily escalate moderate anger into destructive rage. Working through our anger of past events can be accomplished in constructive ways, often with a skilled therapist, but venting is not one of those productive approaches to anger resolution. Brad Bushman, coauthor of an extensive review of 154 studies of anger management involving more than 10,000 participants, cautions, "I think it's really important to bust the myth that if you're angry you should blow off steam—get it off your chest. Venting anger might sound like a good idea, but there's not a shred of scientific evidence to support catharsis theory [venting]."[10]

Anger and the desire to lash out at others are choices. Imagine, for instance, that you are stopped at an intersection in your car and another driver "steals" your right-of-way by moving into the intersection before you do. Will you get "righteously" angry? Do you gesticulate and shout at the driver, "You idiot! Are the rules of the road just suggestions for you?" Now imagine what your reaction would be if you saw as you were about to respond that it was your mother driving the car. Would you react the same way? You really don't want to explain to your mom why you flipped her off, do you? We can be righteously indignant, or we can choose to be calm, even amused, by the same stimulus. When white-hot anger erupts, however, you lose the ability to see another person's perspective that might lead to conflict resolution.[11] Rage overwhelms your ability to think straight so consumed are you by your anger.

There are several ways to defuse and deescalate anger, both your own and others, but venting your anger will do the opposite. *Try these suggestions for managing your own anger:*

1. *Reframe self-talk.* Reframing the way we perceive personal slights, judgments, and a host of negative reactions from others can diminish anger before it has a chance to inflame it.[12] How do you get inside someone's head to determine intentionality? If someone trips you, was it intentional or accidental? If the tripster instantly apologizes to you, would you still become very angry, or would you see it as an inadvertent mistake unworthy of an angry response? Instead of assuming negative acts were intentional, assume they were unintentional until proved otherwise. "He just made a common human mistake." "She didn't mean to hurt my feelings. She might have been talking about someone else. I should check."

2. *Refuse to be defensive.* Defensive communication such as criticism and incivility can ignite angry passions. Exercise control over your emotions. Refuse to become defensive. Look for the underlying causes of the criticism or incivility, and confront the criticism or incivility assertively to seek ways to transform the defensive communication into supportive communication.

3. *Consciously calm yourself.* The age-old advice to count to 10 when you first feel your anger bubbling up inside actually works.[13] A longer calming period may be required in serious cases. Usually, there is a 20-minute total recovery period once an adrenaline surge is spiked by anger.[14] Extensive research shows that a key to anger management is to engage in calming activities such as yoga, and slow, deep breathing while concentrating on reducing your heart rate. Also, there is meditation and muscle relaxation exercises (tensing and relaxing), and the avoidance of arousal-increasing activities such as jogging, boxing, and cycling.[15]

4. *Don't rehearse your anger.* You can't change your history of ugly breakups or mistreatment at a job from which you were wrongfully fired. Distract yourself when such negative reminiscences emerge. Play a video game, peruse social media for cute pet videos, or contact a friend to talk about something completely unrelated.

Don't attempt to implement all four of these suggestions simultaneously. Pick one and work on learning it until it becomes virtually automatic. Then you can attempt a second suggestion and so forth.

When venting anger comes from another person, not from you, steps need to be taken to quell the eruption. Dialogue cannot take place when participants are venting. Social media verbal combat exhibits this so often that it is difficult to find a civil conversation online when controversy emerges. *Try these suggestions to defuse another person's anger and restore a climate conducive to dialogue.*[16]

1. *Embrace asymmetry.* When a person is exhibiting anger, particularly if it turns to venting rage, it is important that you do not respond in kind. Be *asymmetrical*—you do the opposite. Neutralize rage with absolute calm, as hostage negotiators are trained to do. "I hear what you're saying, and I want to help solve this problem. Can we just talk about this?" Reciprocating rage is counterproductive. Rage times rage equals rage squared, and that is inviting catastrophe.

2. *Employ the validation technique.* There are several ways to validate another person. You can *apologize*. "I'm sorry. You're right to be angry" can very powerfully validate the other person. Don't apologize, of course, if you should be viewed as blameless. A *compliment* can defuse another person's anger: "I actually think you handled my anger constructively." Finally, *actively listening* to a person who expresses anger and trying to understand their concerns can be very validating.

3. *Encourage a problem orientation.* Asking questions to ascertain what the angry person would like to occur can short-circuit the anger. Probing questions can transform an emotional outburst into a rational pursuit of problem-solving because it requires a thoughtful response. "Do you have a solution?" activates the brain, not the adrenal glands.

4. *Disengage if all else fails.* This step is particularly important if the person continues to be abusive and enraged. Simply and firmly state, "This meeting is over. I'm leaving. We'll discuss this another time."

Concentrate on one or two of these steps until they become second nature to you. Embracing asymmetry is listed as the first step because it is the most critical. The remaining steps can be learned gradually unless physical threat is immediate and disengagement is self-protective. A person can feel angry for excellent reasons. Anger acts as a signal that changes need to occur. Anger should not, however, be used as a weapon to abuse others. We need to learn ways to cope with and express anger constructively, not be devoured by it. Don't embrace the myth that venting your anger is constructive.

Part III

THE GROUP EXPERIENCE

🕚

MYTH: GROUP MEETINGS ARE LIFE-SUCKING BLACK HOLES

When was the last time someone said to you, "I sure wish we had more meetings"? Never? Former Xerox executive Thomas Kayser suggested why meetings have such poor public relations: "A meeting is a place where you keep the minutes and throw away the hours." Columnist George Will once sardonically offered this unsolicited opinion that dovetails with Kayser's viewpoint: "Football combines the two worst things about America: it is violence punctuated by committee meetings." You may disagree with Will's dislike of football, but there is copious evidence that supports his and Kayser's assessments of meetings. A Harris poll reported that 46% of the 2,066 respondents would endure "any unpleasant activity" rather than attend meetings, with 18% picking a trip to the DMV if it would avoid attending meetings, 17% choosing to watch paint dry, and 8% preferring a root canal.[1] Jeff Haden, contributing editor to *Inc.*, emphatically agrees in his essay titled "Why 99 Percent of All Meetings Are a Complete Waste of Money and Time."[2] His 99% figure, however, is merely a made-up hyperbolic overstatement supporting only that *inefficient and poorly organized group meetings* can be a waste.

Group meetings don't have to be perceived with the same dislike one might have for the return of disco. Nevertheless, common complaints associated with group meetings include the following: the purpose for the meeting is ambiguous, meetings are disorganized, participants are distracted by their attention to social media, attendees are unprepared to make constructive contributions, important members are absent or tardy, meetings do not begin on time and they often go overtime, discussion becomes aimless and unproductive, some participants become stage hogs and dominate the conversation and stifle discussion, and critical decisions made at meetings are not implemented.[3]

The pervasive spread of virtual meetings necessitated by the COVID-19 pandemic just added to the disenchantment. College classes were conducted mostly online. Virtual meeting attendees reported feelings of exhaustion and dread when classrooms and boardrooms took solely to the virtual platform during the pandemic.[4] "Zoom fatigue" emerged and cries of wasted time proliferated. Both in-person or online meetings can produce *meeting recovery syndrome*—grousing and complaining about bad meetings that can linger for hours and stifle productive work.[5]

Despite the general disgruntlement associated with group meetings, "Meetings-R-Us."[6] Business executives devote, on average, 23 hours a week to meetings, not including casual "drive by" in-person confabs.[7] Employees attend an average of 62 meetings per month. In an average large company, 300,000 hours are devoted to scheduling and attending meetings.[8] *Meetings are an unavoidable vital part of successful group decision-making and problem-solving when conducted competently.*[9] Meetings permit essential communication processes necessary for competent decision-making and problem-solving to occur. Participants can share vital information, brainstorm new ideas, and finalize agreements. The myth that meetings are a time waster and that groups would be better off jettisoning the very idea of holding meetings except in the most exceptional cases is nourished by poor execution of meetings too often experienced by participants. Bad meetings produce bad outcomes and dissatisfaction with the very idea of gathering for a meeting both in-person or virtual. Nevertheless, some of the most innovative and spectacular solutions to critical problems have resulted from productive group meetings. The Apollo 13 near disaster, for example, the story of which was so dramatically told in the 1995 Oscar-winning film of the same name, was avoided by a group meeting to brainstorm ways to save the spacecraft and its inhabitants. *Synergy*—group performance from joint meetings that exceeds the performance of individuals working alone—requires collaboration, and that requires group meetings. We're not going to get to Mars by "lone geniuses" sequestering themselves from working with other brilliant minds.

Efficient and effective group meetings can neutralize the common misperception that almost all group meetings are a waste of time and should be avoided. Adequate preparation is critical. This is primarily a facilitator's responsibility. *Only call a meeting if there is a clear, compelling purpose.* Don't call a meeting just to disseminate information or to audition new ideas that could be done efficiently by email, phone call, or text message. Schedule a meeting if an immediate response is important on a significant issue or proposed decision, group participation is advantageous, participants are well informed and prepared to consider issues critically and coherently, and key players are available to attend.

Once you have decided that a meeting is required, the meeting's purpose determines who to invite, what to discuss, and how to discuss it. The *purpose* is the measurable result that needs to be accomplished by meeting, such as to generate ideas, solve a problem, or make decisions. Accomplishing such purposes of group meetings necessitates a carefully planned, structured decision-making and problem-solving process.

John Dewey described a process of rational decision-making and problem-solving called *reflective thinking*—a set of logical steps that embraces the scientific method of defining, analyzing, and solving problems.[10] The *Standard Agenda*, derived from Dewey's reflective thinking, is a structured process composed of steps that guide what could be a series of meetings if the problem being addressed is especially complex and volatile. It focuses on a full analysis of the problem before considering solutions, thus eschewing the propensity of groups to jump to solutions before carefully analyzing the problem or issue at hand.

The Standard Agenda consists of the following six steps to solve problems and make decisions in a series of productive group meetings:

1. *Identify the Problem*. The problem should be presented as an open-ended question. For example, "What characteristics make a company worthy of being included on the "best businesses list?"
2. *Analyze the Problem*. To determine which are the "best companies to work for," Michael O'Malley and his colleague, Bill Baker, spent 3 years researching companies featured in business publications such as *Fortune* and *Inc.*[11] They interviewed executives, met with human resources departments, conducted employee focus groups, and toured facilities of the 21 organizations that perennially appeared on several "best companies to work for" lists. From their research, they were able to ascertain criteria that revealed why these organizations are deemed "best companies."
3. *Establish Criteria*. Standards used to evaluate decisions and solutions to problems are called *criteria*. Groups should establish criteria for assessing the quality of solutions before solutions are offered. Criteria are sometimes apparent by edict (e.g., the legal criterion of "beyond a reasonable doubt" in a felony case). Not all criteria, however, should be treated equally. Some criteria are not as relevant or appropriate as others. For example, ranking businesses based on CEOs' salary size, number of employees, availability of parking spaces at the business site, and annual profits and stock performance won't likely get you on the "best places to work" list if that is the goal. The ordinary worker won't reap the rewards of generous CEO salaries, high profits, or rising stocks. A strong wages and benefits package, positive workplace climate, bosses who empower workers and exhibit empathy and emotional intelligence, and reasonable working hours for employees would certainly be better criteria from an employee's viewpoint.

When groups apply different comparative criteria, however, the results can be significantly different. For example, University of Oregon, my alma mater, in 2023 was ranked #98 on the list of top colleges in the United States by *U.S. News & World Report* but #337 by Niche, an educational ranking service. The criteria used by these two sources explain the huge differences in rankings. Top criteria used by *U.S. News* included graduation rates and performance, first-year retention rates, peer assessment, financial resources per student, and faculty salaries.[12] Niche criteria included student academic grades, student loan amounts, alumni earnings, faculty awards, student-faculty ratio, diversity of student body, and student surveys regarding faculty quality.[13]

4. *Generate Possible Solutions*. The group brainstorms possible solutions, or in the "best places to work" case, specific actions that could be taken to meet criteria. Some suggestions for meeting the criteria such as positive workplace climate and strong benefits package for "best companies" could include treating birthdays as paid holidays; engaging in social events such as monthly outings to baseball games, comedy clubs, or theater shows; and organizing summer barbecues, holiday parties, and teambuilding exercises, among other possibilities. Also, establishing programs to assist employees in advancing their careers, such as paying workers to take college classes in business and communication, is another possibility.

5. *Evaluate and Select the Best Solution*. Match the potential solutions to the criteria to assess their quality and feasibility. Evaluation based on criteria may reveal that some of the potential solutions mentioned earlier may not be financially feasible. Others may not be deemed effective, such as teambuilding exercises often perceived by employees to be "funishments"—those "rare and artificial teambuilding exercises that people are forced to take part in and required to enjoy."[14] Paid holidays typical of union-based work and myriad desirable social events would likely be well received.

6. *Implement Solutions*. Groups may choose potentially effective solutions to problems, but too often they don't plan for implementation of their decisions. Failure to do so faces two possible challenges that can disrupt even great choices. First, Murphy's Law—the adage claiming anything that can go wrong likely will go wrong, somehow, somewhere, sometime—can lead to solution failure. For example, not making a digital backup copy of an important report is flirting with Murphy's malevolet adage.

A second challenge recognizes that change can be an ordeal. Overcoming resistance to change requires consideration of three factors—*degree*, *rate*, and *desirability of change*.[15] Large, undesirable, rapid change produces much more resistance, typically, than relatively small, desirable change instituted slowly so organizations can adapt. Just mention sudden and rapid "reorganization" of a department within a company and watch employees freak out.

Finally, there are a few remaining communication tips regarding how to keep meetings efficient and smooth-running affairs. First, *establish simple ground rules for all meetings*, such as "turn off phones," "start every meeting on time," and "no multitasking." Virtual meetings especially should have this as a firm rule because multitasking during Zoom meetings can be more obvious when participants are pictured on a screen fussing with a stack of papers or perusing their phones for all to see. Second, *enforce the no-stage-hogging rule*. Ask each group member to embrace the acronym WAIT ("Why Am I Talking?").[16] This avoids what researchers term the *babble effect*—endlessly just filling the airwaves with aimless discussion.[17] If babbling occurs, any member can interrupt and ask that discussion return to relevant agenda items. Third, *encourage relevant participation from all attendees*. Nonparticipants are dead weight. Finally, *end meetings on time*. When you embrace and execute the steps discussed that carefully structure effective meetings, the myth that almost all meetings are a waste of time and money disintegrates.

16

MYTH: LEADERS ARE BORN NOT MADE

What comes to mind when you think of a leader? Are there certain traits, such as decisiveness, charisma, and courage, that emerge? This traits approach to leader competence is a popular view. Even academic research, as I will discuss, for decades tried to determine which traits make good leaders. *This view sees leadership as a person, not a process.*[1] Thus, the search for "heroic" and extraordinarily talented persons to idolize as iconic examples of desirable leadership became the focus.[2] This perspective has produced some odd results. Among a list of thousands of books on *leaders* and *leadership* available on Amazon are eclectic and sometimes bizarre treatises on such disparate individuals as Eleanor Roosevelt, Barack Obama, Margaret Thatcher, Malcolm X, Ida B. Wells, Gandhi, Volodymyr Zelenskyy, Sheryl Sandberg, Steve Jobs, Attila the Hun, Genghis Khan, Napoleon Bonaparte, Osama bin Laden, and Santa Claus (not kidding).

The stubbornly persistent belief that traits determine leader effectiveness and "leaders are born not made" is a myth.[3] *Traits* are relatively enduring characteristics exhibited by a person that spotlight distinctions between individuals and that are consistently displayed in a variety of contexts. There are physical traits such as height, weight, physique, beauty, and attractiveness; personality traits such as being extraverted, friendly, or shy; inherent traits such as intelligence and quick-wittedness; and traits related to redundant behaviors, such as trustworthiness and integrity.

No small effort has been exerted to identify key traits that likely produce effective leaders.[4] Reviews of hundreds of studies, however, found that there is no universal set of traits that strongly corresponds to effective leadership.[5] Likewise, the Gallup Organization studied 80,000 world leaders covering a span of 25 years and found that they do not share a common set of traits.[6] This should not be surprising. A trait such as intelligence or articulateness could be neutralized by arrogance, ethical indifference, or emotional detachment. Remember the negativity bias (Chapter 11).

Competent leadership does not reside in the person but requires communication transactions that resonate between leaders and followers.[7] A leader with no one willing to follow is like a conductor without an orchestra just delusionally waving a baton. Leaders and followers engage in a symbiotic relationship similar to ballroom dancers. One person leads and the other person follows, but each is influenced by the other. They must work in tandem, or they will appear to be stumbling drunks on a binge. Thus, *leadership is primarily a process, not a person.*[8]

Some traits may be necessary but not sufficient to be a competent leader. Being intelligent and socially adept instead of ignorant and a social disaster certainly seems preferable. Traits alone, however, provide more of a caricature of competent leadership than a revealingly accurate picture.[9] Yet typically we develop prototypes in our minds of strong and capable leaders who should possess essential traits, such as decisiveness, self-confidence, and attractiveness. These prototypes are called *implicit theories of leadership.*[10] Tomas Chamorro-Premuzic, in his wonderfully thoughtful book *Why Do So Many Incompetent Men Become Leaders?*, notes that "people tend to equate leadership with the very behaviors—overconfidence, for example—that often signal bad leadership." He further notes that charisma, although a poorly defined subjective characteristic, is universally perceived to be "a key ingredient of leadership talent." Based on a treasure trove of research, however, he calls this the "charisma myth." He explains that "the most effective CEOs were not charismatic but were remarkably persistent and humble. They excelled not at self-promotion but at nurturing talent in their teams."[11] Acclaimed management expert Peter Drucker long ago concluded that effective leadership "has little to do with 'leadership qualities' and even less to do with 'charisma.'" He further remarked that many effective leaders renowned in history possessed no more charisma "than a dead mackerel."[12]

The misguided traits perspective on leadership effectiveness can reveal some startling results. One study found that almost 4% of 200 business executives studied were *psychopaths*[13]—"someone who has no conscience and feels no remorse or empathy."[14] More recent research, however, found that an even more disturbing 12% of corporate leaders are psychopathic.[15] Whether it is 4%, 12%, or something in between, these are power-crazed, toxic bosses, not cold-blooded killers.

It may seem difficult to accept that anyone who qualifies as psychopathic could ever emerge as a leader. Nevertheless, the research shows that such individuals do attain leadership positions far more often than one might think possible. How do psychopathic individuals gain leadership positions? Initially, they are usually charming, self-confident, decisive risk takers, and articulate. They project an image of a strong leader that meshes with common implicit theories of leadership. Nevertheless, psychopathic leaders are domineering, ruthless, manipulative, and ethically challenged individuals whose toxic communication creates negative workplace climates.[16] These negative qualities, however, may not become obvious until after the psychopath has solidified their formal position of authority.

Continuing the alarming prospect of toxic individuals emerging as nominal leaders when implicit theories of leadership centers one's focus on the traits perspective, there are also narcissists who frequently assume leadership positions in the business arena. *Narcissists* are those individuals who exhibit "a grandiose sense of self-importance; arrogant behavior or attitudes; a lack of empathy for others; a preoccupation with fantasies of unlimited success or power; . . . [and] a desire for excessive admiration from others."[17] Unfortunately, "Narcissists fit our conventional stereotype of what a good leader should look like."[18] They are extraverted, self-confident, decisive, even charismatic. They are especially successful emerging as leaders of new groups that have not had enough opportunity to observe and experience the narcissist's dark side.[19] Narcissistic leaders, however, can diminish worker performance.[20] This occurs because they lack concern for others, create negative work environments, and hinder collaboration in teams.[21] They want control not collaboration.

The troubling emergence of psychopathic and narcissistic leaders in the world of business underlines an essential point: *those who emerge as leaders will not necessarily become effective leaders.* Both psychopathic and narcissistic leaders are power-hungry, Me-oriented individuals, not We-oriented team players. "Psychopathic and narcissistic leaders are often perceived as charismatic, and their followers can be blind to their toxicity."[22]

Departing from the myth of the traits perspective on leadership, "Extraordinary leadership is the product of extraordinary communication."[23] A survey of 1,400 leaders, managers, and executives reported that what is most critical for effective leadership is the ability to communicate competently, and "the biggest mistake leaders make" is inappropriate communication.[24] High on that list of incompetence is *poor listening* or what Daniel Goleman calls "the common cold of leadership."[25] He notes that "poor listening has become epidemic" in the workplace, especially among those in formal leadership positions. *Active listening* requires focusing on others, not on oneself, and seeking understanding, not planning rebuttals. Note that the word *listen* is an anagram for the word *silent* (same letters, different words).

An enormous Gallup study of more than 20,000 senior leaders and more than 1 million work teams aimed at learning the keys to effective leadership concluded that *to be an effective leader you must emphasize your communication strengths and improve in areas of communication weakness.*[26] To accomplish this involves remaining flexible by playing a variety of constructive informal roles, not rigidly remaining fixed on only certain roles that provide comfort from repetition. There are a wide variety of constructive informal (non-designated) roles.[27] There are *task roles* that function to increase the productivity of a group to achieve its goals. Key examples include the following:

1. *Information giver*—provides facts and opinions; offers relevant and significant information based on research, expertise, or

personal experience. "I have this report I found on this very subject . . ."
2. *Initiator-contributor*—provides ideas; suggests actions and solutions to problems; offers direction for the group. "Maybe we should consider our first idea again, but from a different angle."
3. *Devil's advocate*—gently challenges prevailing viewpoints in the group to test and evaluate the strength of ideas, solutions, and decisions. "So, what happens if our plan doesn't play out as we hope it will? Do we have a backup strategy, or are we just hoping for a miracle?"

There are *maintenance roles* that function to gain and maintain a positive group climate. Key examples include the following:

1. *Supporter-encourager*—offers praise; bolsters the spirits and goodwill of the group; provides warmth and acceptance of others. "Great job everyone."
2. *Harmonizer-tension reliever*—maintains the peace; reduces tension with gentle humor; reconciles differences between group members. "Let's try not to make this personal, and perhaps we need to take a break. I think we are growing weary."
3. *Gatekeeper*—controls the channels of communication, keeping the flow of information open or closed depending on the social climate of the group; encourages participation from all group members and open discussion. "We haven't heard from many of you. Any suggestions that you'd like to make?"

Leadership viewed as a shared responsibility, not the sole responsibility of a single individual, is demonstrated when any member steps in and assumes whatever task or maintenance role is required at a significant moment that has not been filled by any other member.[28] This shared responsibility is called *distributive leadership*. This perspective clearly embraces the view that competent leadership is more a process than a person who, in some cases, may operate with the title of "leader" but who may not have a clue how to communicate competently in such a position of influence.

Informal roles unfold dynamically in the context of group discussion, debate, and disagreement. When a group member dominates discussion, for example, any other member needs to become a gatekeeper and silence the disruptive gabster (e.g., "Let's hear from other members, and let's also agree to keep our comments short so everyone has an opportunity to speak"). When the group appears ready to make a specific decision, but no discussion has occurred about potential disadvantages of such a decision, then there is a need for someone to play devil's advocate ("I think this plan has several possible problems that we should consider seriously before taking action"). *Any member can exercise leadership in a group, not just someone designated as the CEO, board chair, chief negotiator, manager, and the like.* One minute you may be an information-giver and the next you may switch to harmonizer–tension reliever depending on the flow of the group's interactions. During a single group meeting you may play many constructive roles, but that shows leadership.

Conversely, exhibiting communication competence as a critical element of effective group leadership requires the avoidance of disruptive informal roles. *Disruptive roles* function to prevent groups from achieving goals. Typical disruptive roles include the following:

1. *Stage hog*—seeks recognition; monopolizes discussion and prevents others from expressing their points of view; wants the spotlight. "Listen to me! I'm not done yet."
2. *Fighter-controller*—tries to dominate the group; competes mindlessly with group members; abuses those who disagree; picks quarrels, interrupts, and generally attempts to control group proceedings. "You're kind of slow to catch on, aren't you? Try keeping up if you can." This is a bully.
3. *Cynic.* This role is a climate killer. A cynic displays a sour outlook, engages in faultfinding, focuses on negatives, and predicts group failure ("We're never going to agree on a decent topic"). H. L. Mencken described a cynic as someone who "smells flowers [and] looks around for a coffin." When the group may need a *cheerleader*, the cynic becomes a *jeerleader* by providing a disheartening message ("I told you we wouldn't succeed. This was a stupid idea").

To review briefly, communication competence is at the heart of leadership effectiveness, not some mythical constellation of traits. The traits perspective is woefully inadequate in providing insight regarding how to perform as a competent leader. Remember, leadership is more a process than a person. Real leaders play many roles in a group or organization. Flexibility is essential.

⓱

MYTH: WOMEN ARE LESS QUALIFIED TO BE LEADERS THAN MEN ARE

A survey of 1,000 Americans asked respondents to name a well-known woman in a leadership position in the world of technology. At the time (2018) they could have named Ginni Rometty (CEO of IBM), Safra Catz (CEO of Oracle), Meg Whitman (former CEO of Hewlett-Packard), or Sheryl Sandberg (longtime COO of Facebook), among others. Respondents had no difficulty identifying prominent men in such positions of power past and present (Steve Jobs, Elon Musk, Bill Gates, Mark Zuckerberg, for examples), but 92% couldn't name a single woman in a similar position, but embarrassingly, digital assistants Siri and Alexa were named by numerous respondents.[1] The situation beyond just the world of technology shows a consistent pattern of men dominating the top power positions in large corporations. Although *more than half* of all mid-level professional and management positions in the United States are held by women, they held just 10.4% of Fortune 500 CEO positions in 2024, actually a record.[2] Fortune's Global 500 list of the largest companies in the world includes 29 women, 5.8% of the total, who serve as CEOs. That's a dismal number, but it is also a record.[3] The numbers for S&P 500 companies are similarly disappointing. Women held CEO positions in 8.2% of these large corporations.[4] For women of color, the results are just depressing. Only 1% of CEO positions in Fortune 1000 companies had a woman of color at the helm in 2023.[5] "Women, women of color, women born outside of the United States, and LGBTQ+ women are underrepresented."[6] At the current pace, the United States will have established a fully functioning human colony on Mars before gender equity in high-level corporate power positions becomes a reality. Women, however, have achieved one milestone. For the first time ever, there were more female CEOs at S&P 500 companies in 2023 than male CEOs *named John*, a dubious achievement.[7]

So is this proof of gender bias? Maybe women are not as qualified, on average, for high-level positions. That is a common myth, but compelling research refutes this notion. Consider just a small sample. Women earn the majority of college degrees, and this hasn't varied since 1979.[8] In the workforce, women with college degrees are more plentiful than men with college degrees.[9] Women consistently perform better than men on leadership capabilities tested.[10] One study, based on more than 240,000 "complete leadership profiles," concluded that women are more effective leaders than men on all leadership measures.[11] "Decades of studies show women leaders help increase productivity, enhance collaboration, inspire organizational dedication, and improve fairness."[12]

Given these results, why do well-qualified women often not rise to the top of the corporate hierarchy? As previously noted in Chapter 12, almost half of women who are sexually harassed in the workplace quit their jobs or change careers. That interrupts their chain of experience to compete for top-level positions. Also, unlike men, women with children are considered less reliable and committed to their jobs, a myth that persists but is contradicted by plentiful research.[13]

Even when women show resilience in what can be the corporate Hunger Games, gender stereotypes can be an added barrier to career advancement. "Archetypal leadership characteristics such as authoritativeness, decisiveness, and directness are typically coded as masculine, which means that women who demonstrate them appear to be violating gender expectations and are often characterized as difficult to work with or temperamental."[14] Thus, as a comprehensive study indicates, women are "more likely to be shunted into support roles rather than landing the core positions that lead to executive jobs."[15]

Additionally, the male-dominated work culture often stifles female communication, giving them less opportunities to visibly shine. *New York Times* columnist Susan Chira notes, "Academic studies and countless anecdotes make it clear that being interrupted, talked over, shut down or penalized for speaking out is nearly a universal experience for women when they are outnumbered by men."[16] Organizational psychologist Adam Grant concurs, "It's usually men who won't shut up. Especially powerful men."[17] He cites research that identifies the tendency of men in groups to engage in *"manologues,"* their usurpation of discussion that leaves little room for women to offer contributions. When a lone woman is in a group of five members, for example, she averages 40% less speaking time than *each* of the four male group members. When four women outnumber the only man in the group, however, the speaking time for each female member equals the speaking time for the lone man. To gain equal airtime during group discussion, women often have to greatly outnumber men. Additionally, *hepeating* is a term that identifies yet another challenge for women. It is the propensity of men to dismiss or derogate women's contributions in meetings but then later to repeat the exact same ideas as their own brilliant contribution. Thus, men get the recognition by seizing quality ideas from women.

Slowly, painfully so, the wholly discredited myth that women are not as qualified or as capable of running major corporations and serving in high-level executive positions erodes. Crushing this myth is an important step in boosting opportunities for women of all ethnicities. Steps to counter gender bias need to be taken. *Amplification*—"echoing and supporting one another's [women's] points and publicly giving one another credit"—is an important step.[18] Amplification by expressly noting a point or contribution made by a female participant, acknowledging its practicality, can short-circuit domineering manologues. Men who are in positions of power, until greater gender equity is achieved, also need to be *allies for women* by creating collaborative, supportive group climates that nurture female leadership advancement.

Women, of course, are not helpless to address gender bias in corporate America. Suzanne Peterson and her colleagues conducted 30 years of research involving more than 12,000 executive leaders. The result of this extensive research strongly suggests that women use a "blended style of leadership" to counter bias. "Women must walk a narrow tightrope: they must have the courage to interrupt, use fewer nonfluencies, and use more intense words while blending in more relational and empathetic responses."[19] These researchers "wish this weren't the case." Dealing with the reality of persistent gender bias thwarting women's career advancement, however, means that the *blended style of leadership* can be a benefit as an interim step until gender equality is eventually realized. A blended style, however, does not mean women should be timid and avoid asserting their points of view. Challenging hepeating, for example, in an assertive not an aggressive manner, is one way to disrupt the men's club at work. "Gee, Gus, I seem to remember suggesting that very solution just a week ago and you ridiculing it. Nice to see that you changed your mind." Finally, women who have cracked the glass ceiling also should reach down and offer a helping hand by acting as *mentors* to less powerful women. This can assist them in rising to more powerful leadership positions and actualize gender equity swifter than we establish a colony on Mars.

Part IV

PUBLIC SPEAKING

18

MYTH: ONLY A NATURAL GIFT OF GAB MAKES AN EFFECTIVE PUBLIC SPEAKER

There is prodigious power in the mastery of public speaking. It is an art that permeates a broad spectrum of society that includes law, politics, teaching, religion, public relations, and business. Competent public speaking enhances self-confidence, improves critical thinking, develops researching skills, bolsters academic performance, and permits greater civic engagement as an influential participant. Political protests large and small almost always require competent public speaking to boost attention to a cause and stimulate enthusiasm for often protracted mass movements to gain a strong foothold in the popular consciousness. One survey found that 92% of respondents believed that "presentation skills are critical to success at work."[1]

Harvard professor Carmine Gallo, author of *Talk Like TED* , notes that, despite being "your key to success in any field,"[2] public speaking proficiency can seem to be relegated to the few individuals who are born with a special talent for such communication. As Gallo notes, however, "One of the most stubborn myths about public speaking is the belief that people who command a stage are naturally gifted. That's nonsense. They've worked at it."[3] As legendary football coach Vince Lombardi once said, "The dictionary is the only place that *success* comes before *work*. Work is key to success." Not everyone can become a superstar public speaker just by working at it, but virtually everyone can become competent public speakers with concerted effort even if initially just the thought of speaking to an audience large or small terrifies you.

Consider my experience. As a child, I was almost pathologically shy. In eighth grade, my teacher apparently thought it would be a great end-of-the-year educational assignment for every student in her class to give a 5-minute speech on one of the presidents of the United States. I thought she was just inhumane. I dreaded making a fool of myself and suffering derision from my classmates. Unable to concoct an escape plan, I agonized for two weeks in anticipation of my feared rhetorical doom. I carefully composed my speech on Ulysses Grant and practiced it repeatedly. I managed to give my 5-minute speech, anxious throughout but relieved that I didn't embarrass myself. I also secretly pledged that I would never give another public speech ever again.

My parents had other plans. Their idea of tough love was to insist that I join the high school debate team my freshman year to help me overcome my shyness. I was flabbergasted. Seeing no way to avoid their insistence that I join the debate team, after much whining and complaining, I attended the first debate team meeting. I was quickly partnered with a first-year student named Jack who was equally reticent to participate. So we devised a strategy to sabotage our parents' plan. We would be so inept in our first debate that our parents would recognize their mistake and allow us to quit the team. Our first and only practice debate went according to our plan. We were thoroughly thrashed by a terrific girls' team.

Embarrassed but weirdly triumphant, Jack and I expected our respective parents to read our judge's ballot with its numerous negative comments about our pathetic performance and release us from our torment. Our plan failed. Our parents just encouraged us to "simply do your best." Jack and I agreed that continuing to humiliate ourselves wasn't exactly a brilliant strategy after all. We decided to request help from our school's senior team and our coach. As a result, I began as a nervous novice debater, gradually managed my fear of public speaking, honed my skills, became a very successful debater and public speaker, and evolved into a speech communication professor and college debate coach. The same diligence can also bring almost anyone similar success.

My initial fear of public speaking is a common problem shared by millions of people, and it can prevent those who experience it from learning the myriad benefits of public speaking excellence. Mark Twain once remarked, "There are two types of speakers: those who are nervous and those who are liars." Overstated perhaps, but public speaking anxiety is pervasive. A survey by Chapman University reported that 62% of the 1,500 respondents feared giving speeches.[4] Another study of college students found that 64% feared public speaking.[5] Others have claimed an even higher percentage.[6] COVID-19 ignited *Zoom performance anxiety*—the added fear of presenting speeches in the somewhat uncomfortable and awkward online platforms.[7]

Speech anxiety can be either dysfunctional or functional. *Dysfunctional speech anxiety* occurs when its intensity prevents an individual from giving a speech effectively. The Chapman University survey already cited provides some measure of the intensity. It reports fear of public speaking as greater than fear of heights (61% of respondents), drowning (47%), flying (39%), and, yes, zombies (18%).[8] As dysfunctional as speech anxiety can be, *its intensity has often been wildly exaggerated.* Some surveys, for example, have reported that many people fear public speaking more than they fear death.[9] Comedian Jerry Seinfeld puts this in perspective: "This means to the average person, if you have to go to a funeral, you'd rather be in the casket than doing the eulogy." *These "death before public speaking" survey findings, however, simply promulgate a myth.*[10] In the highly unlikely event that anyone would be forced to choose between death or giving a public speech, who would choose death? Wouldn't you rather filibuster to delay or even prevent threatened death until possible rescue? Nevertheless, intense speech anxiety should not be glibly discounted. Speech anxiety can become highly dysfunctional for a large percentage of people.

Functional speech anxiety occurs when the fear is managed and stimulates an optimum presentation. If your honest attitude is: "I don't care about these people and I really don't care about giving this speech," then anxiety is not likely to emerge, but such indifference isn't typically a desirable goal. Moderate anxiety can energize you and stimulate a more dynamic presentation.[11] So, if on a scale of 1 to 10, with 1 being apathetic and devoid of anxiety and 10 being curled up in a fetal position in a corner of a room rocking in abject terror while muttering incoherently to yourself, about a 3 or 4 level of anxiety on this scale is appropriate to keep speech anxiety functional.

Understanding what causes speech anxiety can provide insight regarding how to manage it constructively so it is functional, not dysfunctional. Specific causes of speech anxiety fall into two general categories. The first category is *self-defeating thoughts*—a person's excessive concern that their audience will judge and reject them if their speech exhibits any flaws. Turn down the volume of your dysfunctional, negative self-talk.[12] Don't catastrophize. Don't predict total failure from a simple opening flub. "Oh no, I stumbled during my very first sentence. What a disaster!" No, it isn't unless you permit yourself to fall victim to such a self-defeating thought.

Speakers can also amplify their anxiety by failure to recognize the myth called the *illusion of transparency*—the self-defeating thought process in which you overestimate the extent to which audience members detect your nervousness.[13] As difficult as it may be for you to accept, research shows that your anxiety is not likely to be apparent unless it is greatly exaggerated.[14] You can become "nervous about looking nervous" but usually for no good reason.[15] Recognizing that your speech anxiety is not likely to be obvious to an audience can actually reduce your anxiety.[16]

A second cause of speech anxiety is *anxiety-provoking situations*—a constellation of contexts that can trigger fear. The *novelty* of the speaking situation may precipitate speech anxiety because the context is unfamiliar from lack of experience. As you gain experience speaking in front of groups, you gain a reservoir of knowledge regarding how to handle almost any situation that might occur when speaking to an audience.[17]

Being conspicuous, or the *center of attention*, is also an anxiety-provoking situation for public speakers.[18] Gaining confidence from experience speaking often to a variety of audiences is a strong antidote for managing speech anxiety provoked by this "spotlight effect." Similar to the illusion of transparency, there is a common tendency to overestimate the extent to which listeners are judging you while you speak.[19]

Finally, *types of speeches* presented can be a situational trigger for anxiety. Telling a simple story to a group of classmates may produce little or no anxiety, but giving a lecture as a teaching demonstration while interviewing for an important job isn't comparable. Suddenly being asked to "say a few words" with no warning can jump-start your anxiety whereas giving a more prepared speech can be far more comfortable.[20] Then there is the challenging task of giving a speech to an audience hostile to your expressed point of view. This may trigger considerable anxiety, but presenting in front of a highly supportive audience can be exhilarating and fun.[21]

Self-defeating thoughts and anxiety-provoking situations that can produce speech anxiety can be managed. Many individuals, from famous actors and celebrities to so-called social media influencers, have suggested strategies for managing speech anxiety. The list includes swearing at your audience backstage or just before initiating your Zoom connection, and sticking a pin in your backside (pain as diversion). Then there is the oft-repeated suggestion to imagine members of your audience naked or clothed only in their underwear or in diapers, a disturbing image that is more likely to distract you if not make it difficult to stifle your amusement. There is no good evidence that any of these suggestions are truly effective at dampening speech anxiety. *They qualify as myths*. If there were compelling evidence, speech instructors everywhere would be distributing pins to their anxious students, encouraging them to poke their backsides before delivering a speech while handing out paper towels to mop up the blood. These are diversionary tactics rather than serious strategies to address the principal causes of speech anxiety.

So, what does work? *Preparation and practice are essential*. Careful preparation reduces the novelty and uncertainty associated with the speaking situation. Don't delay starting your research, organizing and outlining your speech (see Chapter 22), and practicing your presentation. Practice your speech repeatedly until it becomes very familiar.

Gaining proper perspective is another effective strategy for managing speech anxiety. *Proper perspective* is the straightforward formula: *the severity of the feared occurrence times the probability of the feared occurrence.*[22] Severity can vary from mild symptoms such as the feeling of butterflies in the stomach, perspiring slightly, momentarily forgetting a point you planned to make, and occasionally stumbling over words to more extreme symptoms such as flop sweating, knees shaking uncontrollably, mentally freezing, and even vomiting. Now to gain perspective, imagine that the most severe symptoms, the entire mess occurs. How would you react? Would you hide from friends and family? Would you quit your job, ashamed to show your face to your colleagues at work who witnessed the unfortunate event? Would you leave the state and join a monastery, taking a vow of silence? Realistically, none of these melodramatic reactions would be your choice. Yes, you would very likely feel embarrassed, even very disappointed, but that is about as severe as the consequences are likely to be. Now regarding probability, embrace the reality that *predictions of public speaking catastrophes are highly unlikely to occur.* I listened to more than 20,000 student speeches as a college professor. I witnessed some unimpressive, decidedly uncomfortable presentations, but only a minuscule number qualified as unforgettable disasters. No student vomited, fainted, or shook violently. The few disaster cases consisted of behaviors such as wildly off-topic rambling, inarticulate delivery, forgetting parts of the speech, and pacing like a leopard in a zoo cage. The apparent cause in every instance, however, was an obvious lack of preparation. The students didn't "work at it."

Aside from a very small sample of individuals who experience panic attacks in circumstances much broader than just public speaking, catastrophic failure should not be a concern. Among the thousands of students who took my public speaking classes, only *one* had to address real panic attacks, and even in this instance, we found ways to overcome his challenges with generalized anxiety so he could eventually give his presentations to his class.

One final strategy to manage speech anxiety is to stop focusing on yourself and *focus on your audience.* This is called the *communication orientation*—concentrating on making your message clear and interesting to your listeners.[23] Choking under pressure occurs most often when you view your speech as a performance to be evaluated. You scrutinize your presentation as you deliver it (e.g., "vary your voice," "use strong eye contact," "don't pace," etc.). This misplaces the focus on you instead of on your listeners. When compared to other methods of speech anxiety management, research shows that *the communication orientation is the most successful.*[24]

Virtually anyone can learn to become a competent public speaker. No one is born a silver-tongued orator. That is just a common myth. Speech anxiety, however, deters huge numbers of people from developing powerful public speaking skills. Learning to manage speech anxiety is an important first step toward developing public speaking excellence.

⑲

MYTH: SOME PUBLIC SPEAKING TOPICS ARE HOPELESSLY BORING

How compelling would you think a speech on how to tie your shoes properly is likely to be? Boring topic, right? Trivial and just silly. Now check out Terry Moore's TED Talk on YouTube appropriately titled "How to Tie Your Shoes," and you may come to believe that maybe there are no boring topics. *The myth is that many topics are perceived to be just inherently boring and tedious and cannot be made interesting.* This may seem true at first blush, especially if a topic is highly technical and complex. Assuming that certain topics cannot be made interesting no matter what you try, however, is surrendering to defeatism when knowledge and use of key attention strategies can likely invigorate almost any topic.

Depending on your audience, of course, what sparks interest, even excitement, in one group of folks may not so easily overcome initial disinterest in a different audience. For example, a conference composed of geotechnical engineers will likely find meticulous presentations on the topic of new slope stability assessment options interesting, even exhilarating. For the layperson, however, this may seem capable of inducing a coma. Audiences pay little attention to that which does not interest them. Thus, capturing attention is imperative to maintaining listeners' focus on a topic.

The nature of attention is a transactional process in which speakers and listeners work together to create a captivating experience. Attention is intrinsically selective. You cannot focus on more than one stimulus at any moment.[1] Thus, *attention* is the act of concentrating on a single stimulus to the exclusion of competing stimuli. Here lies the predicament for any speaker. Minds are easily distracted.[2] ("I don't have a short attention span. I just . . . Oh look, a squirrel!") Given that we are bombarded daily by stimuli vying for our attention at any moment (see Chapter 4), how do speakers keep the focus primarily on their topic and messages? To expand the point, how do you not only grab immediate attention of your audience during your speech introduction but also maintain that attention throughout a lengthy presentation? It is noteworthy to get off to a fast start by seizing listeners' attention. Ignoring the far more challenging task of keeping that focus, however, can be similar to a sprinter flying out of the starting blocks but slowing to a crawl a few meters into the race.

The speaker has the primary task of generating an audience's attention, *so it is almost always the speaker who is boring, not the topic.* Listeners, however, also play an important role in this transactional communication process. Have you ever watched comedians who desperately struggled to get their audiences to laugh? It's difficult to watch. My wife and I attended a semifinal for the annual San Francisco Comedy Contest a few years back. One of the 10 contestants struggled mightily to engage his listeners. About 4 minutes into his performance that should have lasted 10, he stormed off the stage, cursing at his audience. Ironically, the very next contestant had this same audience convulsing in uproarious laughter. He won the semifinal and ultimately the final contest later. The unsuccessful comic was not nearly as skilled as the winning comic. It wasn't the topic but the execution that resulted in comedic failure.

The success of any speech is dependent on the audience's perspective, not some sacred list of pure criteria for speech effectiveness set in stone. "I gave a stellar speech (or comic routine), but the audience despised it" mimics "The surgery was a huge success, but the patient died" analogy. Think of audience analysis as the process of speakers discovering ways to identify with listeners' needs, hopes, interests, and concerns, and for listeners to identify with speakers. *When your audience can identify with you, gaining and maintaining listeners' attention and topic interest is more likely.*

Identification is the affiliation and connection between speakers and their audiences. We identify more closely with those individuals who seem to be similar to us than those who are not.[3] *Stylistic similarity* attempts to create identification between a speaker and their audience by looking and acting as listeners look and act. In June 2009, comedian Stephen Colbert visited American troops stationed in Iraq. He dubbed his series of comedic performances *Operation Iraqi Stephen: Going Commando*. Demonstrating the power of stylistic similarity to captivate attention, Colbert paraded onto the stage wearing a camouflage business suit and tie. The height of his effort to identify with his military audience occurred when General Ray Odierno shaved his head to exhibit solidarity with the soldiers. The soldiers roared their approval. One soldier, Ryan McLeod, summed up the prevailing view, "Definitely the highlight was seeing him sacrifice his hair."[4]

A second way to build identification and foster audience attention is to align your opinions, values, and attitudes with those of your listeners. This *substantive similarity* establishes common ground. If listeners can say, "I can relate to what I'm hearing," they can identify with the speaker and remain positively attentive. If you are speaking to a hostile audience, referencing common experiences, perceptions, values, and attitudes should occur before addressing contentious sources of disagreement. Failure to do so may provoke negative attention in the form of heckling or worse.

A third way to establish identification with an audience is *storytelling*. In the world of effective attention strategies, storytelling is unsurpassed. Substantial research shows that storytelling promotes *social cohesion*—it binds us together in mutual liking.[5] "Storytelling is one of the few human traits that are truly universal across culture and through all of known history."[6] Everyone seems to enjoy a story well told and likes the artful storyteller. "We humans have been communicating through stories for upwards of 20,000 years, back when our flat screens were cave walls."[7] Our brains respond "with more focus and engagement when we hear stories than facts."[8]

Stories can be short vignettes or highly involved narratives. Terry Hershey is a Protestant minister and a master storyteller who for more than three decades has presented enormously popular lectures at the annual Religious Education Congress in Anaheim, California. Here is his classic story that he often tells at this conference to make the point that we learn in childhood to fear making mistakes:

> There's a terrific story about a first-grade Sunday school class. The children were restless and fussy. The teacher, in an attempt to get their attention, said, "Okay kids, let's play a game. I'll describe something to you. And you tell me what it is."
>
> The kids quieted down. "Listen. It's a furry little animal with a big bushy tail, that climbs up trees and stores nuts in the winter. Who can tell me what it is?" No one said anything. The teacher went on. "You are a good Sunday school class. You know the right answer to this question. It's a furry little animal with a big bushy tail, that climbs up trees and stores nuts in the winter." One little girl raised her hand. "Emily?" "Well, teacher," Emily declared, "it sounds like a squirrel to me, but I'll say Jesus."[9]

Every time Hershey tells this story, his audience erupts with laughter.

Here is how you tell an effective story to gain and maintain attention when giving a speech[10]:

1. *Ensure story-audience compatibility.* A story about the challenge and strategies of playing blackjack at a casino will not likely resonate with an audience that abhors gambling. You don't want to draw attention to a repellant message if possible.

2. *Align story with your speech purpose.* Stories should advance your speech purpose not just entertain, unless entertaining is the point of your presentation.

3. *Utilize the three main structural story components: challenge, struggle, and resolution.*[11] Terry Hershey's story has a challenge (guess the right answer), a struggle (kids attempting to deduce the correct answer), and a resolution that provides a moral to the story (the fear factor).

4. *Practice telling your story.* Rehearsing your story is important. You want to sound natural, not artificial. A poorly told story creates negative attention.

5. *Be animated, even visual, when telling a story.* A story usually needs to be told dynamically. It may benefit from acting out certain parts. Dynamism can powerfully enhance listeners' attention.

A fourth way to build identification with an audience is to use *humor*. As a stellar attention strategy, humor is a close second to storytelling. "We've childproofed our house, but they keep finding a way in" is an ironic unattributed quip that has been circulating on the Internet for decades because its humor garners lasting attention. Actor Ryan Reynolds, as does Terry Hershey, loves to combine humor with storytelling, therefore using two attention strategies together. For example, during an interview he tells this brief story: "Usually when I'm on an airplane with my kids, at some point I get up and ask the flight attendants if I can leave the aircraft. Ninety-nine percent of the time they say, 'No, please stay seated!' So, I just sit back down and long for the sweet release of death."[12]

Using humor effectively, however, can be challenging. Chirpy advice such as "Be funny" isn't helpful. Appropriateness and effectiveness are complex issues that are always present. Here are basic guidelines for employing humor competently as an attention strategy:

1. *Do not force humor.* Don't humiliate yourself if friends and relatives groan every time you try telling a joke and you predictably flub the punchline. You can, however, use the humor of others. Quips such as the African proverb: "Unlike the brain, the stomach alerts you when it's empty" can be quoted to make a point about the importance of education and the dangers of ignorance. Amusing occurrences related by others can also be useful. Avoid a risky lead-in, however, such as "I heard the funniest story yesterday" or "My kid said the most amusing thing." If your audience doesn't find it funny, the silence can be awkward.

2. *Humor must be relevant.* Irrelevant humor that is disconnected from the purpose of a speech or a main point dangles unproductively. Connect the humor directly to a main point or central theme. Here is an example: "New York Yankees manager Casey Stengel once ordered his players to 'line up alphabetically according to your height.' Actress Brooke Shields once tried

sounding profound with this remark: 'Smoking kills. If you're killed, you've lost a very important part of your life.' We've all done it, said something that comes out as nonsensical and triggers derisive laughter. But when our most powerful leaders from the president on down make such statements, it can have international repercussions, as I will show throughout this presentation." The humor is straightforward, and it introduces the purpose of the speech.

3. *Consider your audience and occasion.* Don West, the defense attorney in a highly publicized murder case, started his opening statement to the jury with a clunky knock-knock joke. The jury was clearly repelled by such insensitivity. Does the grieving family of the murdered victim sitting in the courtroom want to hear a joke that makes light of a horrific personal tragedy? West later apologized to the jury and indirectly to the family. Using humor appropriately can be tricky. Coarse vulgarities, obscenities, and sexist, racist, and homophobic "jokes" can alienate listeners. Unless it is an official "roast," hostile humor should engender caution. Jokes about sex and religion and dark humor do not travel easily across a wide variety of cultures. Collectivist cultures that highly value harmony may deem sarcasm, satire, and aggressive humor offensive.[13] Clever quips and self-deprecating humor, however, do travel well across cultures generally.

Clearly, both storytelling and humor enhance identification with an audience and therefore stimulate listeners' interest. *Novelty* can be added to the list of effective attention strategies. Novelty doesn't work primarily from identification with an audience, however, but instead exploits our natural attraction to that which is new and different.[14] Conversely, the commonplace and repetitive can seem tedious and uninteresting. To grab the attention of airline passengers who typically tune out the standard safety instructions provided before takeoff, flight attendants have on occasion provided safety instructions by, yes, using humor in a novel way. One flight attendant became a YouTube sensation with instructions, such as: "Your seat cushions can be used for flotation, and in the event of an emergency water landing, please take them with our compliments" and "To activate the flow of oxygen (to the mask), simply insert 75 cents for the first minute." Avoid starting a speech with a mundane attention killer, such as: "My topic is . . ." Stimulate interest in your topic with a novel introduction. Even better, choose a *novel subject* if given a choice. ChatGPT can be helpful in providing possible interesting and novel topics.[15]

There are many additional ways that novelty can attract attention. *Novel wording* is widely recognized as a great attention-getter especially when businesses choose a name for their establishment. Here are a few possibilities:

- Curl Up and Dye (hair salon)
- Broken Egg (breakfast restaurant)
- To Thrill a Mockingbird (pet store)
- Waste Not, Want Not (septic disposal)
- Nailed It (nail salon)

Follow the example of businesses cleverly naming their establishments. *Colorful phrasing or unusual wording* can transform an ordinary statement into a memorable one, even serve as a cleverly worded theme for your speech. For example:

Ordinary: My workplace is depressing.
Novel: "My office has started random urine testing of employees to detect traces of hope or optimism." (unattributed Twitter tweet)
Ordinary: There are stupid people in the world.
Novel: "The universe consists of protons, neutrons, electrons, and morons" (attributed to rock star Frank Zappa)
Ordinary: I'm very old.
Novel: "At my age, I don't buy green bananas." (Actor James Garner)

You can also add *novel examples* that illustrate important points of your speech. For instance, Dr. Anthony Iton, whose medical degree is from Johns Hopkins University, provides this novel piece of history:

It was an African American who first introduced the underlying concept of vaccination to America in the early 1700s. An enslaved person in Boston named Onesimus explained to his enslaver, Cotton Mather, the process of inoculation or variolation. Variolation was the ancient African practice of taking a small amount of the fluid from an active smallpox skin lesion of an infected person and transferring it to a wound on an uninfected person, thus inoculating that uninfected person. This is the central concept underlying vaccination that is in use today.[16]

"I want to talk to you about the history of inoculations" just wouldn't have an equivalent attention-getting effect as this more novel opening.

Startling your audience with *novel statistics* can be especially compelling as an introduction to a speech. For example, a study of 125 of the world's richest billionaires reports that these individuals have a stake in 183 companies that produce 393 million metric tons of greenhouse gases every year. That is equivalent to the carbon dioxide emissions from the whole of France. This means that each billionaire is responsible for a million times more greenhouse gases than the average person.[17] A less significant yet startling example is provided by science writer Steve Mirsky, in an article for *Scientific American*. He notes that, based on 65 studies, researchers estimate that there are approximately 55 billion pounds of spiders in the world. That is about half the estimated weight of the Great Wall of China. Mirsky quotes American Museum of Natural History arachnologist Norman Platnick with this somewhat unnerving conclusion: "Wherever you sit, a spider is probably no more than a few yards away."[18]

Finally, making a *vital appeal* can be a powerful attention strategy. Audiences tend to heed warnings when a societal problem affects them personally, or if they think it might. COVID-19 almost immediately became of vital interest to Americans. The effects on our society were tumultuous, and actions to stem the virus were hugely controversial, riveting our collective attention almost daily for years. Widespread mask wearing and shelter-in-place edicts reinforced the inescapable personal nature of the virus.

Gaining listeners' attention can be a real challenge. Maintaining that interest during a lengthy speech can be even more daunting. Applying some of the attention strategies I have presented can bolster audience interest. Don't assume that some topics are hopelessly uninteresting. That's just a myth. *Make topics interesting.*

⓴

MYTH: OPEN-MINDEDNESS MEANS OPEN TO ALL POSSIBILITIES

Open-mindedness is often perceived to be inherently good even when such openness can be ridiculous or harmful. *This myth of open-mindedness as inherently and unqualifiedly positive is pervasive.*[1] A common retort made by proponents of controversial claims when challenged is to fire the verbal salvo, "Don't be so closed-minded." A truly closed-minded person, however, is often a *true believer*— someone who accepts claims without solid reasoning or valid evidence and holds tenaciously to these claims even when incontrovertible reasoning and overwhelming contradictory evidence is offered as refutation. Winston Churchill sardonically defined a true believer as anyone "who can't change his mind and won't change the subject." If they want something to be true, then, to them, it is true regardless of the unsupportable nature of the belief. That's closed-mindedness in its strongest version.

Open-mindedness is a desirable quality, up to a point, but it does not necessitate *bothsidesing*—"giving credence to the other side of a cause, action, or idea to seem fair or only for the sake of argument when the credibility of that side may be unmerited."[2] Do you really want to listen to a speaker assert that gravity doesn't exist just to appear open-minded? As the bumper sticker notes: "Gravity: Not just a good idea; it's the law!" *An open mind is not one cluttered with debunked nonsense.* People believed that our Earth was flat (and some still do), that bloodletting cured diseases, and that trephining—a procedure that involved drilling a hole in a live person's skull—released evil spirits thought to cause madness.[3] Not enough has changed, unfortunately, since these earlier times of shared ignorance. In times past, people simply didn't know better because science and data availability were not well developed. Today, there is no excuse. Open-mindedness does not mean reticence to challenge patently false beliefs and assertions just to create an impression of a fair hearing for controversial claims.

Falsehoods are abundant, especially in today's polarized political climate that encourages a fake "openness" to myriad assertions of alleged truths. A RAND research report cleverly dubs the disturbing deterioration of critical thinking practices and the all too frequent tendency of individuals and groups to remain open to wildly false ideas as "truth decay."[4] Famous satirist and author Jonathan Swift long ago noted, "Falsehood flies, and the truth comes limping after it." Results from a study conducted at the Massachusetts Institute of Technology confirmed Swift's view. Fake news was 70% more likely to be shared on social media than real, substantiated news. Accurate information took six times as long as misinformation to reach 1,500 people. Facts rarely spread to more than 1,000 people, but the top 1% of erroneous information routinely spreads to between 1,000 and 100,000 people on Twitter (renamed X). Bots played no part in spreading misinformation. Instead, it was people of every political persuasion, left and right, who were "open" to the novel, surprising, and emotional nature of most false claims.[5]

Open-mindedness should not mean suspending one's critical thinking to accommodate "both sides" on issues and purported events, but when such suspension does occur, the results can be head scratchers. A stunningly ludicrous example of minds "open" to irrationality was offered by extremist group QAnon followers. They asserted that our assassinated president John F. Kennedy faked his death and was still alive even though he would have been 104 years old when, as claimed, he would appear with his dead son, John Jr., on November 2, 2021, at Dealey Plaza in Dallas, Texas, the site of the assassination. It gets more bizarre. John Jr., a lifelong Democrat and progressive and victim of a tragic, fatal plane crash on July 16, 1999, would supposedly become Donald Trump's vice-presidential running mate in 2024 (oops, missed that one when J. D. Vance actually became Trump's running mate and subsequent vice president). Hundreds of true believers gathered expecting the younger Kennedy's grand appearance along with his centenarian father. When this delusional event unsurprisingly did not materialize, QAnon devotees in many cases stayed for months waiting in hopeful anticipation that the prophecy would eventually come true. They remained "open-minded" despite the failed prophecy.[6] There is no bothsidesing this strange event. There is only one rational side.

The same is true for most conspiracy theories. Political polarization in recent years and the emergence of the COVID-19 pandemic have produced countless *conspiracy theories*—explanations of social and political events or circumstances usually involving secret plots that are unlikely to be true based on an impartial examination of empirical proof. A national survey by the Carsey School of Public Policy at the University of New Hampshire found that a significant minority of respondents exhibited "openness to conspiracy beliefs."[7] Lest you think that conspiracy theories are primarily promulgated by right-wing conservatives, a common recent viewpoint, an exhaustive analysis of voluminous research on a wide variety of conspiracy theories concludes otherwise.[8] *Although some conspiracy theories are more favored by conservatives than liberals and others the reverse, overall neither conservatives nor liberals have a corner on the conspiracy market*.[9] This same research shows, for example, that slightly more liberals than conservatives believe that the moon landing was a hoax. A Chapman University survey reported that 24% of participants believed the moon landing was faked.[10] Consider the "truth decay" necessitated by this one conspiracy theory. For the U.S. government to have faked the moon landing, 411,000 NASA employees would have had to be partners in the conspiracy,[11] none of whom has ever admitted engaging in such fakery. The Soviet Union, our Cold War nemesis at the time, carefully monitored the Apollo missions and was racing the United States to the moon. If the moon landing had been faked, the Soviet Union would have trumpeted it to the world. There is no "other side" on the moon landing and no requirement that such nonsense be entertained to appear open-minded. What this research on conspiracy theories shows is that, when it comes to uncritical open-mindedness, political ideology is no safeguard.

Being open to "both sides" even when there is only one logical position can produce obvious irrational contradictions. As conspiracy theories researcher Joseph Uscinski notes, "There are studies where you ask people, 'Do you think Osama Bin Laden is still alive, or do you think he was dead before the Navy Seals got to him?' And you find a bunch of people who believe both, which is impossible."[12]

So, what does it mean to be open-minded if it does not mean entertaining any claim someone makes no matter how far-fetched and illogical? *"What truly marks an open-minded person is the willingness to follow where evidence leads."*[13] This requires an understanding of what elsewhere I have called the *probability model*.[14] Claims vary in degrees of likelihood from *possibility* to *plausibility* to *probability*, and at its most extreme, *certainty*. For practical purposes, we can rule out certainty as a useful claim to advocate. Few things in this world are certain. Death and your dryer will eat your socks qualify, but little else (OK, JFK and John Jr. are definitely dead). Decision-making and problem-solving are best based, not on possibility alone or even plausibility, but on high probabilities because the probability model is an open system of thinking.[15] Even our most treasured beliefs about the universe, for example, may someday prove to be imperfect and subject to alterations small or even large. Let me explain the model in some detail.

Clearly, arguing solely from possibility is problematic. The statement, "Don't be so closed-minded; it's possible" can lead you down a treacherous path. It is possible that your immune system can fight off a fever of 105 degrees triggered by an infection without emergency medical intervention, but why would you take the chance? Get to a hospital, pronto. "Anything is possible" is insufficient justification for gambling with your life. "Possibility" can also lead to gambling addiction, disastrous investments, and a host of other poor decisions based on hope and desperation.

Conversely, excessive concern for your safety based only on possibility is likewise weak thinking. For example, is it likely that you might contract COVID-19 from fleeting exposure with an infected person? Babak Javid, an infectious disease physician at the University of California, San Francisco, doesn't rule out the possibility, but he explains: "I am not going to say it is impossible. I think the risk of, you know, someone cycling past you and giving you COVID is minimal, to say the least."[16] Don't anguish about highly unlikely events.

A claim based on plausibility is stronger than one centered on possibility alone. This is because plausibility requires a logical basis. When new viruses emerge, only the most plausible theories on how to combat them will likely gain federal grants to conduct research. Implausible theories (e.g., eat lots of chocolate) provide no rational basis for distributing scarce resources for research to find cures. Assessing the plausibility of a claim has become increasingly essential with the burgeoning use of artificial intelligence (AI) and ChatGPT, technology that is alarmingly capable of pumping out disinformation and misinformation that can seem plausible but is erroneous.[17] That's why *plausibility alone is not a strong enough basis for accepting a claim.*

Plausibility, however, can be a basis for investigation of unresolved questions. Is it plausible considering the vastness of the universe that organic life exists elsewhere besides just on Earth? Yes, it is plausible, but it remains an open question devoid of strong supporting evidence to confirm such a conclusion. Nevertheless, SETI (Search for Extraterrestrial Intelligence) is a scientific organization that has researched space in an effort to answer the question of whether intelligent, organic life exists elsewhere in the universe. Plausibility can be a logical basis for investigating what we don't know but hope to find out.

Claims based on plausibility, however, can seem logical but can lead us astray. For example, the *correlation as causation fallacy* is a prime example. A *correlation* is a consistent relationship between two variables. A *variable* is anything that can change. Causal claims (x causes y) based on correlations (x occurs and y also occurs either sequentially or simultaneously) alone can initially seem quite plausible. A common example is the correlation that you get a flu shot and the next day you are sick from the flu. It can seem plausible that the shot caused the flu or they are totally ineffective, but flu shots are derived from a dead virus and they do not create strong immunity for typically two weeks after the shot so it is very likely that you already were exposed to the virus and the vaccine's immunity boost hadn't kicked in yet.[18]

Finding even a strong correlation between two variables does not prove causation, and as psychologist and author of *Rationality* Steven Pinker concludes, "Almost any causal conclusion you draw from correlations . . . is likely to be wrong, or at least unproven."[19] Although some correlations can seem quite plausible as causations at least on the surface, Tyler Vigen, in his book *Spurious Correlations*,[20] cites numerous implausible correlations. For example, there is a strong correlation between per capita consumption of cheese and the number of people who died by becoming tangled in their bedsheets. The divorce rate in Maine correlates with the per capita consumption of margarine. The marriage rate in Kentucky correlates strongly with the number of people who drowned after falling out of a fishing boat. Correlations can suggest plausible causation, and that can be an important starting point for further investigations, but correlations alone are insufficient reasons to claim *probable* causation.[21]

A strong argument requires moving beyond just plausibility. The higher the probability the stronger is the argument. Probability, however, for a single event doesn't necessarily generalize to a larger sample.[22]

With more than eight billion people in the world, weird things will occur to some of them. This demonstrates the law of very large numbers—with large enough numbers, almost anything is likely to happen to somebody, somewhere, somehow, sometime.[23] On June 8, 2009, a small boy was hit by a meteorite but suffered only minor injury. Given that thousands of meteorites hit the ground each year, the probability of someone, somewhere, at some time being struck by a meteorite is high.[24] The probability that *you* might be struck, however, is infinitesimal despite the single example of the boy being struck. It's possible but extremely improbable. Don't lose sleep over it.

Thus, high probability for a claim is not established by arguing from example. When individuals jump to a conclusion based on a single or a handful of examples, especially vivid ones, they have committed a *hasty generalization fallacy*.[25] Consider the mass media's tendency to sensationalize each new scientific study that gets published. This is especially true when pharmaceutical companies tout their latest and greatest drug (with corresponding lists of sometimes startling and even stomach-churning side effects, including potential death). A single study, however, is insufficient to draw any general conclusion. In science, studies are replicated before results are given credence because mistakes can be made.

The more extraordinary the claim, the greater the requirement for extraordinary evidence.[26] If your claim requires rewriting the laws of physics, for example, your evidence must be way beyond just ordinary. That is why paranormal phenomena require much stronger evidence than has been produced so far to accept their existence.[27] The evidence supporting them is meager, controversial, and unconvincing.[28] As a 12-year study of 3,800 predictions clearly shows, self-identified psychics have an 11% accuracy rate. Educated guessing should be more accurate.[29] To make this point, I predicted the winners of six ongoing national presidential races in each year that they occurred as a demonstration in my college classes before the final two principal party nominees were chosen. I was correct in five of the six races for an 83% accuracy rate. In five of those races, I even correctly predicted the exact percentage difference in popular votes between the two main candidates in final vote tallies. The one presidential race that I predicted the wrong winner I fell within what I jokingly called "the psychic margin of error." (Psst! I have no psychic powers; or should I be open-minded about the possibility that I do and just don't recognize my powers?)

Ultimately, *open-mindedness necessitates an assessment of the probabilities of any claim.* It requires judgment and critical evaluation. Follow where credible reasoning and evidence leads. You exhibit open-mindedness when you are willing to examine new information. Too often, however, confirmation bias rears its troublesome head. *Confirmation bias* is the tendency to seek information that supports one's beliefs and to ignore information that contradicts those beliefs. Studies show that confirmation bias is pervasive.[30] Individuals generally do not spot faulty claims because they search for and listen to assertions and information that support their beliefs, and they ignore contrary information. It can be disquieting to expose oneself to information and evidence that disrupts cherished or strongly held beliefs.

Self-correction of faulty claims should be embraced, not resisted. Be open-minded to where reasoning and evidence leads, not to any claim even if thundered from the rooftops by a majority of people. As a line popularized by astronomer Carl Sagan noted: "You don't want to be so open-minded that your brain falls out."

21

MYTH: EXPERTS CAN BE WRONG SO WE SHOULDN'T VALUE THEM

Tom Nichols, author of *The Death of Expertise*, warns: "I fear we are witnessing the death of the ideal of expertise itself, a Google-fueled, Wikipedia-based, blog-sodden collapse of any division between professionals and laypeople, students and teachers, knowers and wonderers—in other words, between those of any achievement in an area and those with none at all."[1] He adds: "Ignorance has become hip, with some Americans now wearing their rejection of expert advice as a badge of cultural sophistication." Nichols quotes Isaac Asimov, who wrote about anti-intellectualism in the United States that nurtures the "false notion" that "my ignorance is just as good as your knowledge." *The "experts don't matter" myth has become a dangerous trend.*

To denigrate experts is to become a victim of the *illusion of explanatory depth* that nurtures this dangerous contempt for experts. Too often individuals and groups harbor this illusion that they know more than they do, so who needs experts?[2] So instead of seeking advice from medical doctors who spend years studying disease and potential cures, those who repudiate experts tout superficially acquired medical "wisdom" from "the University of Google." Battles over vaccine efficacy and safety, heated exchanges regarding advice and direction from the Centers for Disease Control and Prevention about COVID-19, and climate change debates, among other incendiary issues, have under-lined controversy concerning the significance reliable experts play in matters of life and death.

Yet, we want a surgeon to perform a difficult procedure on us to remove a dangerous tumor, not someone who dabbles with cutlery and has seen the procedure performed on a YouTube video. When stepping into an elevator, we assume that proper, regular safety checks and maintenance have been completed by those in the know. We trust experts to prevent us from plummeting to our death. We would be foolish to trust the hotel concierge's confident assessment that the hotel elevators are "perfectly safe."

Nichols explains why experts should be highly valued: "Experts are the people who know considerably more on a subject than the rest of us and are those to whom we turn when we need advice, education, or solutions in a particular area of human knowledge."[3] Experts are not infallible, but the probability that their knowledge and advice can provide us with useful and correct counsel on complex matters is far higher when compared to someone who is not a relevant expert. Experts can help laypeople sort fact from fantasy, and this is no small assistance. As Thomas Jefferson once wrote: "If a nation expects to be both ignorant and free in a state of civilization, it expects what never was and never will be."

So, how do you determine expertise and whether an expert is reli-able or biased, because experts do not necessarily agree on controver-sial issues?

1. *There are three criteria to qualify as a true expert.* You look at the person's knowledge, skill, and achievement. This is made credible by considering their education, experience, and dem-onstrated competence in their field. "Experts are not always perfect. Experts do make mistakes, but they're also ready to catch their own errors and eager to learn from them."[4] If an expert makes serious mistakes, don't jettison all expert advice, just find better experts. The most reliable experts are those who correct their infrequent mistakes as evidence requires. They let their data, not just their opinion devoid of credible data, lead to their conclusions.

2. *Don't quote experts outside their field of expertise.* An expert in one field is not an expert in all fields. Having a doctorate doesn't confer expertise in unrelated subjects. As Tom Nichols explains, "Experts can go wrong, for example, when they try to stretch their expertise from one area to another. This is not only a recipe for error but is maddening to other experts as well."[5] A marine biologist is not an expert on software engineering. An English literature professor, by virtue of their education, is not an expert on virology. A business consultant is not an expert on communication and interpersonal relationships. Experts may disagree, but are they all speaking in their field of expertise?

3. *Consider source credibility.* Sources of expertise must go beyond just individuals in this digital age. Be very careful accessing ChatGPT (AI—artificial intelligence). "ChatGPT will cite papers that don't exist . . . and it continually provides false and misleading references."[6] This may become a more consistently credible source of expert information in the future, but exercise caution. Also, the specific source of information on the Internet is not always clear from accessing a website. Are you looking at medical information from the Mayo Clinic or from a misinformed blogger sipping a brew while posting clickbait to thousands of equally misinformed followers? If no source is apparent other than the name of a website, be very suspicious. Even an author's name without accompanying credentials should ring warning bells. You may be able to find the credentials of an author by consulting EBSCO's *Biography Index Past and Present*, or there may be a link to the author's home page. Try typing the author's name in the Google search window. This may reveal whether the person has strong credentials or is a sketchy source associated with biased or questionable affiliations. If you can't verify an author's credentials, don't use the source. Check to see if references are cited in the article and make a quick check of some of them to see if they exist or are from reputable publications.

4. *Look for complete, recent source citations.* Every statistic that is not mere common knowledge (e.g., there are 50 U.S. states), every controversial assertion of facts, and any testimony of asserted

experts used to support claims should have a credible source. Otherwise, dangerous nonsense can parade itself as significant truth. Unlike an essay or journal article, audience members listening to a presentation do not typically have access to a bibliography. So, you must provide sufficient information orally to build credibility. Credible source citations should include, as a minimum:

a.   the *name* of the source,

b.   the *qualifications* of the source if not obvious,

c.   the *specific publication* or media citation where the evidence can be found, and

d.   the *relevant date* of the publication.

Evaluate the source and its qualifications and also determine whether the source is recent or out of date. Recent source citations are usually more credible on most subjects. Also, don't accept a source as a credible expert just because it agrees with your opinion (remember confirmation bias).

5. *Look for source bias.* Two Stanford University studies found that most student participants could not recognize the bias of various sources of information.[7] If a source engages in a hard sell to peddle products, therapies, or ideas, you should view it with suspicion about its accuracy because there is the inherent bias of the profit motive. *Look for sources that have no vested interest, no profit motive, and no axe to grind.* Public-interest groups such as Consumers Union (publishes *Consumer Reports*), the American Cancer Society, and Common Cause have long-established reputations for providing impartial, credible research-based information. Most *political claims*, especially when made in the heat of a political election, can be checked for accuracy at nonpartisan sites such as *PolitiFact*, considered a solidly reliable source for truth analysis by a careful academic study.[8]

6. *"Beware before you share."*[9] Irina Raicu, director of the Internet ethics program at Santa Clara University, offers this advice: "Most people are not misinformation experts. . . . We are all, however, potential participants in the spread of disinformation." She continues by encouraging everyone to recognize the danger of ChatGPT "AI-generated disinformation" and resisting the dissemination

of "truth decay" by posting and reposting "messages that seem to demonstrate exactly what some people believe." Don't share before you have made a concerted effort to confirm the truth and validity of information by checking additional, credible sources.

The denigration of experts has become a serious national concern. The more we devalue expertise the greater is the likelihood that bad, even catastrophic decisions will be made. Don't fall victim to the "experts can't agree so ignore them" myth. You can always find disagreement among experts, but the prevailing view among most or almost all experts usually leads us in correct directions.

22

MYTH: EFFECTIVE SPEECHES REQUIRE A MANUSCRIPT

TED Talks (TED stands for Technology, Entertainment, and Design) have become enormously popular, especially since videos of these presentations began to be posted online in 2006. The TED Commandments, a list of guidelines given to TED speakers, includes this one: "Probably the worst of all public speaking sins is the temptation to disappear into your notes and read, as opposed to speak, to your audience. If they wanted to be read to, you could've just sent them an email with your speech content."[1] *It is a myth that to give an effective speech you must construct a precise manuscript*, yet a cursory search on the Internet shows abundant websites touting how to "write an effective speech." *If you write it, you will read it*. The temptation to read from a manuscript, despite the best intentions to only glance at the written composition, will be too strong to resist.

It is very difficult to deliver a scripted speech that can connect with an audience and engage listeners. I could always tell without looking as I wrote my critiques whether a student in my class was reading from a manuscript. There is a discernable rhythm when someone reads, and it can sound like Siri announcing why she cannot access your playlist. Reading from a manuscript can markedly distract from your message.

I offer one caveat: *a manuscript speech may be an appropriate method of delivery in very limited situations.* If precise phrasing is critically important as a safeguard against accidental slips or gaffes that could cause legal complications or trigger nasty audience outbursts, then a manuscript may be warranted. Practically speaking, however, the belief that almost all speeches require a manuscript so the speaker doesn't simply forget important points or make verbal mistakes is a myth in almost all situations.

There are several significant drawbacks to manuscript speeches. First, *smooth digressions from a prepared manuscript can be very difficult, especially if you are an inexperienced public speaker.* Such digressions, however, may be crucial if an audience does not respond well to your content. Plowing forward with scripted remarks when a speaker's audience is falling asleep or booing at the speaker for taking controversial positions on issues shows failure to adapt to the unfolding circumstances because the speaker is wedded to their script.

Second, *speakers are inclined to read from the manuscript and eye contact with listeners suffers.* Direct eye contact can gain and maintain listeners' attention and interest. Conversely, when you do not look directly at your audience, listeners' minds can easily wander.[2]

Third, *it is difficult to project dynamism when pinned to a manuscript.* Sleepy, monotone, lackluster presentations encourage listless responses from your audience. You want to be dynamic, not lethargic if you hope to excite your listeners. *Dynamism* is the enthusiasm, energy, and forcefulness that a speaker exhibits. Unless you are a trained actor capable of projecting dynamism when performing an audiobook, dynamism will escape you if you read from a manuscript.

Finally, *oral and written style are noticeably different.* A written speech sounds like an essay, not a speech, because the sentences are typically more complex and lengthier than when we speak without a script, and written style is usually more formal with appropriate use of grammar and well-constructed sentences that can be carefully edited. Oral style, the spoken word unfettered from an exact script, tends to be more conversational, and grammatical mistakes may even occur occasionally because sentence construction happens on the spot. Even professional speechwriters composing scripted presentations for political leaders posted on a teleprompter usually strive for "soaring rhetoric" that can easily sound artificial and not well suited to the speaker's personality and way of speaking naturally.

So what about ChatGPT writing your speeches? The question contains its own problem—namely, "writing your speech." ChatGPT can mimic human-sounding language, but it can produce "artificial" style that isn't the way we normally sound delivering an extemporaneous, manuscript-free speech.[3] If ChatGPT is prompted to produce a "formal" style, it can sound pompous and emersed in verbiage. If prompted to produce an "informal" style, it can sound slangy and ludicrously casual, even silly when delivered. Construct your own speech so it sounds authentic for you, and approach your presentation as an extemporaneous speech, not as an orally presented English composition.

An *extemporaneous speech*—delivered from a prepared outline or notes—is the primary alternative to a manuscript speech. This method of delivering a speech has several important advantages. First, *an extemporaneous speech sounds spontaneous* because you don't have the methodical rhythm so often obvious when reading from a manuscript. You glance at a carefully prepared outline, then you put your thoughts into words on the spot. *Extemporaneous speaking also permits greater eye contact and connection with the audience.* Your listeners don't just see the top of your head as you look down while reading your manuscript. Finally, *extemporaneous delivery allows the speaker to respond to audience feedback as it occurs.* You can adjust to the moment-by-moment changes in audience reactions even in virtual speeches given on Zoom if the audience is visible.

The essence of extemporaneous delivery is speaking from an outline, so let's discuss the basics of outlining a speech. Begin by choosing an effective outlining format. You can find many versions on Microsoft Word. The bulleted format is often the first choice, especially for PowerPoint slides. It can become more of a grocery list of seemingly separated bulleted points, however, than a logical outline of quickly discernible interconnected ideas.

Thus, the standard classic outlining form is preferable (also available on Microsoft Word). It uses a *specific set of symbols* that more obviously demarcates interconnected main points clearly and logically from subpoints. Briefly, here is the set of symbols:

   I. *Roman numerals* for main points
      A. *Capital letters* for primary subpoints
      B. Another primary subpoint
          1. *Standard numbers* for secondary subpoints
          2. Another secondary subpoint
              a) *Lowercase letters* for tertiary subpoints
              b) Another tertiary subpoint
  II. Roman numeral for second main point

Visually distinguishing main points from the primary, secondary, and tertiary subpoints is accomplished by *indentation*. Note that you do not logically divide something into just one part. If I'm dividing a whole pie into just one, then I'm keeping the entire pie and you get squat. Therefore, a *minimum of two subpoints* are required to divide a larger, more general point.

Logical consistency and clarity of your outline flows from the specific purpose statement for your speech. A *specific purpose statement* is a concise, precise statement composed of simple, clear language that both encompasses the *general purpose* (i.e., inform, persuade, entertain, demonstrate, eulogize, etc.) and indicates what a speaker hopes to accomplish with the speech. When developing your outline, begin with your general topic, narrow the topic to your specific purpose statement, and further narrow by developing main points from that purpose statement, which break down even further into more specific subpoints. In this way, you work from the most general (over-arching topic) to the most specific (subpoints).

Coherence requires that main points flow directly from the specific purpose statement for logical consistency and clarity. Subpoints also should flow from main points. In Shakespeare's *Much Ado about Nothing*, the character Don Pedro asks, "Officer, what offense have these men done?" The ridiculous constable Dogberry replies incoherently, "Marry, sir, they have committed false report: moreover, they have spoken untruths; secondarily, they are slanders; sixth and lastly, they have belied a lady; thirdly, they have verified unjust things; and, to conclude, they are lying knaves." Dogberry's comprehension of numbers seems to have no coherent sequential meaning. His response is a jumbled mess. *Signposting*—a spoken organizational marker, usually numerical, that indicates the structure of a speech and signals a point about to be addressed—can help provide coherence, especially if subject matter is complicated. Phrases such as "My first point is . . . ," "My second point is . . .," and so forth orally signpost your important points and organize your speech into a coherent whole.

There are several patterns for organizing the body of your speech into an outline. The most common ones are topical, chronological, spatial, problem–cause–solution, and narrative. A *topical pattern* is a good choice when your information can be categorized into types, classifications, or parts of a whole. A topical pattern is often used for *informative speeches*, the purpose of which is to *teach* your audience something new, interesting, and useful, not typical for *persuasive speeches* whose purpose is to *convince* your listeners to change a viewpoint and/or behavior. Here is an example:

GENERAL PURPOSE: To inform
SPECIFIC PURPOSE STATEMENT: To identify different types of humor.
  I. *Humor by mistake* is unintentional humor usually resulting from error.
     A. "I take for granite my landscaper choosing the right rocks for our walkway"
     B. "I'm an English major; your not."
 II. *Ironic humor* is the use of words to imply that the literal meaning is opposite the intended meaning.
     A. "Imagine a documentary about the Flat Earth Society getting a Golden Globe Award."
     B. "There is no greater irony than dying in a living room."
III. *Self-deprecation* is humor that makes fun of yourself.
     A. "I'm only posting on social media so everyone else can feel better about themselves. You're welcome."
     B. "If I remember correctly, the last time I was someone's type was when I was donating blood in the blood drive."
 IV. *Sarcasm* is derisive humor.
     A. "Unless your name is Google stop acting like you know everything."
     B. "Life's good. You should get one."

   V. *Pun* is a play on words in which a humorous effect is produced by using a word that suggests two meanings.
      A. "I'm reading a book about antigravity. It's impossible to put down."
      B. "Becoming a vegetarian is a big missed steak."

A *chronological pattern* suggests a specific sequence of events. One cannot put a roof on a house before pouring the foundation and framing the structure. So, consider this chronological outline, abbreviated (no subpoints):

GENERAL PURPOSE: To inform
SPECIFIC PURPOSE STATEMENT: To explain the expansion of Highway 1.
   I. Construction work will occur primarily from 10 p.m. until 6 a.m. (you should be asleep; enjoy the noise).
   II. This is a two-year project (expect maximum inconvenience; patience required).
   III. Trees and plant growth will be removed along the right side of the highway.
   IV. Excavation and grading a single lane north and another lane south is next.
(Take Steven Wright's advice: "When everything is coming your way, you're in the wrong lane.")
   V. Finally, asphalt and surfacing processes will complete the job.

A *spatial pattern* requires a visualization of where things are located. Here is an example:

GENERAL PURPOSE: To inform (lighthearted)
SPECIFIC PURPOSE STATEMENT: To explain space allocation in the new communication building (with visual aids).
   I. There are five average-size classrooms on the main floor.
   II. There are two second-floor lecture halls where COVID-19 can spread (*still reading?*).
   III. Broom-closet-size faculty offices are adjacent to the large lecture halls.

IV. A student study and meeting facility is located on the second floor with a stunning view of trash bins and cement walls.

V. Student parking spaces will be located in the next time zone.

The *problem-cause-solution pattern* is most appropriate when you explore the nature of a problem and advocate a solution for the problem. Consider this basic example:

GENERAL PURPOSE: To persuade

SPECIFIC PURPOSE STATEMENT: The federal government should establish a subsidized nationwide homeowner's insurance program.

I. Private homeowner's insurance has become widely unavailable or unaffordable.

II. Wildfires, hurricanes, and other natural disasters have made it impossible for private insurance companies to provide affordable coverage.

III. Only a federal government program can make homeowner's insurance available to all at affordable prices.

Finally, speeches are sometimes arranged as a narrative. The *narrative pattern* tells a story, hopefully an interesting one, often in chronological order. The following is an example:

GENERAL PURPOSE: To inform

SPECIFIC PURPOSE STATEMENT: Taylor Swift has evolved into a pop music icon.

I. Swift's childhood was filled with music and singing opportunities.

II. She blossomed as a country musician at first.

A. She won the Academy of Country Music Award for Top New Female Vocalist in 2007.

B. She won additional numerous awards in the country music genre.

III. Her fifth album, which introduced her move into pop music, was released in 2014, and she has rocketed to superstardom ever since.

IV. In 2024, *Forbes* magazine declared her to be the first artist to become a billionaire solely on the basis of her music.

As you become increasingly familiar with your material, especially if you give the same speech more than once, your outline can be compressed into a few words or phrases instead of full sentences, except for the specific purpose statement that should be precisely worded for clarity. This is called a *presentation outline*. Take a look at this example:

I. INTRODUCTION
    A. Attention: Personal story of student debt—my "homeless mortgage"
    B. Significance: 43 million Americans affected—it ain't rich people
    C. Credibility: Extensive research; mother president of large bank
    D. Purpose Statement: Student debt in United States serious and rising problem.
II. BODY
    A. Student debt serious and rising (*Forbes*, April 18, 2024)
        1. $1.75 trillion up from $1.57 trillion in 2018
        2. Average debt: $35,210
    B. Student debt crushing borrowers (Educational Data.org, 2022)
        1. 20 years, on average, to pay
        2. 40% of borrowers may default by 2024
        3. COVID-19 reprieve on paying debt in 2022 has ended
I. CONCLUSION
    A. Summary of main points
        1. Student debt serious
        2. Student debt crushing borrowers
    B. Connect to personal story
    C. Student debt second only to home mortgage

There are other more sophisticated organizational patterns than these, but I have provided the basics. The lengthier your speech, the more detailed will be your outline in concert with your organizational pattern that is appropriate for your specific purpose.

Some speakers attempt to give *memorized speeches* instead of using the extemporaneous style of delivery. This is a manuscript speech absent a visible script. Now you're asking for real trouble. Memorizing a speech of 5 minutes or more is likely to result in you forgetting portions of your speech and standing wordless for what may seem to be an excruciating pause for both you and your audience. Silence isn't golden when giving a speech. Those pregnant pauses can seem like the onset of labor pains, or so I'm told.

A short toast at a wedding, a brief acceptance speech at an awards ceremony, or a few key lines in a lengthy speech may benefit from memorization, especially if what you memorize is emotionally touching or humorous (no one wants the punch line of a joke to be read). For example, "Quoting Ogden Nash: 'To keep your marriage brimming, with love in the wedding cup, whenever you're wrong, admit it; whenever you're right, shut up.'" Aside from these exceptions, memorizing a speech, particularly if the speech is fairly lengthy, is a bad idea even if you have an astounding memory, because all the problems associated with writing a speech still pertain.

An *impromptu speech* is an address delivered on the spot often without any forewarning. It is the antithesis of a manuscript speech. You are asked to respond to a previous speaker or to say a few words on a subject without advance notice. If you have any inkling that you might be called on to give a short speech, begin preparing your remarks. Do not wait until you are put on the spot. You will deliver it off-the-cuff without notes, but your main points are at the ready. Impromptu speaking is not a viable alternative to a manuscript speech, of course, because it is mostly unprepared and very difficult to deliver articulately unless you have had substantial practice. Organizing an impromptu speech is also highly challenging.

Clearly, writing your speech is counterproductive. Using a manuscript invites too many potential pitfalls. It is a myth that effective speeches require a carefully prepared manuscript. Learn to present speeches extemporaneously. Once mastered, you'll never want to write your speeches again (unless you find yourself running for president of the United States and you require a speechwriter, and good luck with that).

23

MYTH: LOGIC AND EVIDENCE ARE THE MOST EFFECTIVE PERSUADERS

Social media posts can sometimes capture the challenge of persuading people to change their minds. For example, consider this post that is dripping with sarcasm: "I hate my job. The work sucks. The people suck. The pay sucks. (Looks up and sees motivational poster on the wall.) Well this changes everything." Television producer Gary David Goldberg long ago sardonically observed, "Left to their own devices, the networks would televise live executions. Except Fox—they'd televise live naked executions."[1] Not much has changed since Goldberg's cynical observation. The graphic, gruesome, and grand event can especially galvanize our attention and influence our attitudes and behavior. This is called the *vividness effect*.[2] A single airline crash, for example, can induce many people to choose driving their automobile instead of traveling by plane. Yet the odds of dying in a plane crash are 1 in 11 *million* but 1 in 5 *thousand* when traveling by car.[3] Logic and evidence may be negated by the single vivid example.

I would like to finish this book with a chapter on how powerfully persuasive logic and evidence can be, given my advocacy of the probability model carefully delineated in Chapter 20 and the importance of expertise and evidence explored in Chapter 21. Unfortunately, the reality is that *attitudes and behavior are rarely changed by logic and evidence alone*, what Aristotle called *logos*, and oftentimes not at all. To believe otherwise is to embrace a myth. This was made abundantly clear when I discussed true believers who are unmoved by refutational logic and evidence piled as high as Mount Everest. Although logic and evidence can be persuasive, especially for highly involved listeners who cognitively wrestle with complex, controversial issues, significant persuasion often requires complementary *emotional appeals*—what Aristotle partially meant by *pathos*. As social psychologist Drew Westen observes, "We do not pay attention to arguments unless they engender our interest, enthusiasm, fear, anger, or contempt. . . . 'Reasonable' actions almost always require the integration of thought and emotion."[4] Unfortunately, the thought part too often devolves into emotional bloodletting between verbal combatants. Debates on Facebook and other social media can quickly deteriorate into the *ad hominem fallacy*—diverting attention from issues raised by attacking the messenger on a personal level while ignoring the message presented: "You're an idiot." "No, you're a moron." And back and forth goes the verbal cage fight without even the veneer of logical argument and evidence.

Aristotle offered a third means of persuasion besides logos and pathos. He explained that *ethos*, or what today we usually call *source credibility*, is also influential, sometimes highly so. Take, for instance, Bell County Kentucky High School valedictorian Ben Bowling's speech that received wide national media coverage. He offered this quotation: "Don't just get involved. Fight for your seat at the table. Better yet, fight for a seat at the head of the table." He attributed the quotation to Donald Trump. The crowd exploded into rousing applause. "Just kidding," Bowling then confessed. "That was Barack Obama."[5] The crowd, in a county that voted 82% for Trump in the 2016 presidential election, went mostly silent with some boos heard. Likely, the reverse could produce a similar response with a quote attributed to Obama in a liberal partisan crowd only to reveal that it was actually from Trump. The source of quotations used to bolster a logical argument can make a big difference. Choose a source poorly suited to an audience, and logic and evidence may be completely ignored.

Persuading those who disagree with you is a complicated process. Consider the relationship between attitudes and behavior. It is illogical for a person to have a pronounced inconsistency between a stated attitude and subsequent behavior. Saying one thing then doing the opposite makes you look hypocritical and irrational. Yet, multiple studies show that attitudes and behavior are often not in sync.[6] An *attitude* is "a learned predisposition to respond favorably or unfavorably toward some attitude object."[7] In other words, you are primed to evaluate stuff. Examples include "Lawyers are dishonest," "Travel is good for the soul," and "True terror is to wake up one morning and discover that your high school class is running the country" (Kurt Vonnegut).

Consistency between attitudes and behavior is influenced by several variables. First, attitudes and behavior usually align closely when influenced by *direct experience*.[8] If you have endured poverty, been unemployed for a significant period of time, or suffered the embarrassment of soliciting money from relatives, friends, or strangers, then this direct experience (personal behavior) likely influences your attitude regarding the propriety of government food stamps, unemployment benefits, and welfare payments for poor people and those struggling to survive crushing debt and the high cost of living. Your behavior toward those similarly afflicted by unfortunate circumstances is more likely to correspond closely with attitudes formed from your direct experience than if you have only indirect "second-hand attitudes" derived from more impersonal media depictions and news articles.[9]

When trying to persuade people, help them *feel* that they are directly affected by the problem you describe while providing credible supporting evidence. Consider this example:

> Failing to vote for Proposition 22 on Tuesday is not an option, unless you don't care whether your college tuition rises 20% next year, and twice that in the following year. Don't expect financial aid to soften the blow because it won't begin to cover the cost increases. According to the Legislative Analyst's Office on its website just last month, more than 500,000 students in this state will drop out of college because they can no longer afford to continue their education. That could be you!

Make your listeners "feel the pain." Logic, evidence, and emotion along with source credibility make a nice persuasive package.

A second variable affecting attitude-behavior consistency is *social pressure*. Valued groups can exert strong influence on our behavior even when logic, evidence, and personal beliefs contradict the group.[10] When someone in a valued group makes a sexist comment, you want to object, but you may remain silent from fear of being branded a "troublemaker" or being socially ostracized as too hypersensitive. Social pressure and fear of disapproval make giving a speech that you know will ignite a negative reaction very intimidating. Arguing logic and providing evidence will likely fall on deaf ears. Remaining silent, unfortunately, may be viewed as the practical choice.

A third variable affecting attitude-behavior consistency is the *effort required to perform the behavior*.[11] For example, you know that being overweight and eating a poor diet is unhealthy. Logically, eating a plant-based diet, exercising, and refraining from alcohol could improve your physical condition, but the effort required to make such changes can be difficult to embrace much less carry out. If your favorite machine during a workout is the television set not the treadmill and you love fatty foods and beer, then the substantial effort can diminish motivation. Reducing that perceived effort can be a key to changing your behavior.[12] Subscribing to online programs that provide healthy already prepared food, working out with friends to make it fun instead of drudgery, and merely cutting back on beer intake all can help in this regard.

The common inconsistency between our attitudes and behavior can make a person appear hypocritical, and research reveals that we strongly dislike hypocrites.[13] An employee asks their boss for more time on an assignment. The boss says no. The employee responds, "But Davis got extra time. How come you won't give me the same extension?" The boss wants to be very fair. Faced with this apparent inconsistency, the boss feels uncomfortable. Psychologist Leon Festinger labeled this unpleasant feeling *cognitive dissonance*.[14]

Cognitive dissonance can be used to influence attitudes and behavior change. As a strategy, you have to awaken dissonance in listeners for persuasion to occur. Psychologist Carol Tavris argues that cognitive dissonance "is as motivating and uncomfortable as hunger or thirst."[15] Here is how the strategy works:

The [persuader] intentionally arouses feelings of dissonance by threatening self-esteem—for example, by making the person feel guilty about something, by arousing feelings of shame or inadequacy, or by making the person look like a hypocrite or someone who does not honor his or her word. Next, the [persuader] offers one solution, one way of reducing this dissonance—by complying with whatever request the [persuader] has in mind. The way to reduce that guilt, eliminate that shame, honor that commitment, and restore your feelings of adequacy is to give to that charity, buy that car, hate that enemy, or vote for that leader.[16]

Although cognitive dissonance can be an effective persuasive strategy, humans have a remarkable facility for rationalizing all sorts of attitude-behavior contradictions that defy logic. The dissonance can be minimized, trivialized, or ignored.[17] "I know it is important to vote in political elections, but my one vote won't matter anyway." Being a couch potato takes precedence.

Two additional persuasive strategies tap directly into the importance of matching logic and evidence with emotional appeals. The first is *fear appeals*, a common parenting practice to keep children safe. "Don't run with scissors"; "Look both ways before crossing the street so you don't get hit by a car." Do fear appeals persuade? In general, research strongly supports the persuasive potential of arousing fear in listeners.[18] The state of Montana experienced an enormous methamphetamine catastrophe among young people. To combat this plague, a barrage of extremely graphic, terrifying video ads of teens hooked on the drug were spread across various media for years. As a result, based on careful follow-up research, teen meth use declined 77% in the state. Subsequently, additional states followed the Montana Meth Model and achieved similar results. In Arizona, teen meth use declined 65%, and Idaho experienced a 56% decline.[19]

Appealing to fear, however, is not a surefire persuasive strategy. *Five conditions must be met to be effective.*[20]

1. *Make your audience feel vulnerable.*[21] We don't all fear the same things. I fear heights and can't even watch Tom Cruise defy gravity in his many stunts in *Mission Impossible* movies and his 2024 Summer Olympics closing ceremony stunt. It makes me dizzy and churns my stomach to watch him hang from skyscrapers. Other

people inexplicably climb steep cliffs and skydive. Some individuals, however, are terrified to give a public speech, but in Chapter 18, I told my story of how I conquered speech anxiety. A poorly aimed fear appeal will fail to persuade listeners because they won't feel vulnerable to the threat.

2. *Offer a specific solution to assuage the fear.*[22] A vague recommendation, such as "Combat climate change," is not as effective as a specific recommendation, such as "Purchase an electric car" or "Install solar panels for your house."

3. *Recommend action that will be perceived as effective.*[23] Scaring people about the potential collapse of the economy and a worldwide depression just creates massive anxiety and feelings of unavoidable doom if no strategy deemed effective to prevent the cataclysm is offered. During the onset of the COVID-19 pandemic, strong steps to stimulate the economy and support workers who lost their jobs prevented an economic collapse in the United States and triggered a subsequent vigorous economic recovery later. This helped assuage the fear of many that crushing debt and poverty were on the horizon.

4. *Recommend actions that will be perceived as achievable.*[24] Again, the effort required to perform the behavior is relevant. Asking members of your audience to give up all sugary foods such as donuts may not be possible for most people. The effort is too great. Encouraging your listeners to cut their consumption in half, however, may be seen as realistic.

5. *Combine high-quality arguments with fear appeals.* The Montana Meth campaign provided abundant statistics on the effectiveness of the campaign. It wasn't just fear appeals unsupported by facts and evidence. The entire campaign was bolstered by research that showed that it was working. Again, *it's the combination of logic, evidence, and emotional appeals that are usually the most persuasive approach.*

Arousing anger is another commonly used persuasion strategy. Double the cost of homeowner's insurance and watch the ire emerge. Cancel a major college football program, then seek shelter in a country with no extradition treaty. Anger can be an effective catalyst for provoking action, even more effectively than fear,[25] but uncontrolled anger can backfire badly. The intensity of the anger is key. Intense anger can short-circuit a person's ability to think cogently and act responsibly (see Chapter 14). You don't want to incite mob violence.

As a speaker, you want to remain calm, be unconditionally constructive in your comments even when others are not, and avoid taunting a heckler in your audience, especially if you are speaking to a hostile audience. Moderate anger can be channeled toward constructive behavior. Rage cannot.

The *Anger Activism Model* helps explain the relationship between anger and persuasion.[26] This model provides three conditions that posit when an anger appeal is likely to be most persuasive:

1. The target audience initially agrees with your point of view.
2. The anger you express as a speaker can be fairly strong but not to the point of rage.
3. Your audience members perceive that there is an effective and constructive action that can be taken to assuage the anger.[27]

Research shows that if all three of these conditions are met, igniting an audience's anger has the potential to motivate appropriate action, even if the action to quell the anger requires considerable effort.[28]

We may wish that logic and credible evidence would be powerful persuaders, but often appeals to emotion serve as critical companions and may be more effective alone in some circumstances. Consistency between attitudes and behavior are not necessarily the result of logical processes. Humans are not automatons. Direct experience, social pressure, effort required to perform the behavior, and source credibility all influence the degree to which behavior will correspond to attitudes.

This completes my journey into the realm of communication myths. This is not an exhaustive compilation and refutation of all communication myths, just the almost two dozen most significant ones. At this point you have realized that just debunking communication myths is insufficient. Exploring the complex process of communication competence as the effective counterpoint to these myths is essential. The extensive discussion of communication competence in its complexity provides what you need to know about human communication while correcting what we know that isn't so.

NOTES

CHAPTER 1

1. Konstantin, D. (2023, January 9). Communication in the modern world. *Linkedin*. https://www.linkedin.com/pulse/communication-modern -world-konstantin-dr-/. See also Norquist, R. (2020, April 5). The basic elements of the communication process. *ThoughtCo*. https://www.thoughtco .com/what-is-communication-process-1689767; Hung, K.-P., & Lin, C.-K. (2013). More communication is not always better? The interplay between effective communication and interpersonal conflict in influencing satisfaction. *Industrial Marketing Management*, 42, 1223–1232.

2. Goleman, D. (1998). *Working with emotional intelligence*. Bantam Books.

3. Howard, L., & Steber, C. (2024, February 20).Experts explain why breaking up over text is so common. *Bustle*. https://www.bustle.com/life/is -it-ok-to-break-up-with-someone-over-text-why-its-so-common-according-to -relationship-experts-7823100

4. Quoted by DeLange, H. (2023, March 3). USD computer science expert dives into ChatGPT. *University of South Dakota*. https://www.usd.edu /academics/colleges-and-schools/college-of-arts-sciences/south-dakotan-arts -and-sciences/usd-computer-science-expert-dives-into-chatgpt

5. Lieberman, M. D. (2013). *Social: Why our brains are wired to connect*. Broadway Books.

6. Anderson, R., & Ross, V. (2002). *Questions of communication: A practical introduction to theory*. St. Martin's Press.

7. Watzlawick, P., Beavin, J., & Jackson, D. (1967). *Pragmatics of human communication*. Norton.

8. Jolly, J. (2023, October 6). Punctuation is "judgey"? Text before calling? How proper cellphone etiquette has changed. *USA Today*. https://www.usatoday.com/story/tech/tips/2023/10/06/new-phone-etiquette-2023/71082660007/

9. Kumar, A., & Epley, N. (2021). It's surprisingly nice to hear you: Misunderstanding the impact of communication media can lead to suboptimal choices of how to connect with others. *Journal of Experimental Psychology: General, 150*, 595–607. https://psycnet.apa.org/doi/10.1037/xge0000962

10. Suttie, J. (2020, November 2). Should you call or text? Science weighs in. *Greater Good Magazine*. https://greatergood.berkeley.edu/article/item/should_you_call_or_text_science_weighs_in

11. Conger, K. (2023, August 3). So what do we call Twitter now anyway? *The New York Times*. https://www.nytimes.com/2023/08/03/technology/twitter-x-tweets-elon-musk.html

12. Wooldridge, M. (2023, May 17). ChatGPT is not "true AI." A computer scientist explains why. *Big Think*. https://bigthink.com/the-future/artificial-general-intelligence-true-ai/

13. King, H. (2023, February 15). Global survey: Worker burnout reaches new high. *Axios*. https://www.axios.com/2023/02/15/burnout-2022-2023-slack-remote-work-future-forum

14. Minkin, R. (2023, May 17). Diversity, equity and inclusion in the workplace. *Pew Research Center*. https://www.pewresearch.org/social-trends/2023/05/17/diversity-equity-and-inclusion-in-the-workplace/

15. Noe-Bustamante, L., Martinez, G., & Lopez, M. H. (2024, September 12). Latinx awareness has doubled among U.S. Hispanics since 2019, but only 4% use it. *Pew Research Center*. https://www.pewresearch.org/race-and-ethnicity/2024/09/12/latinx-awareness-has-doubled-among-u-s-hispanics-since-2019-but-only-4-percent-use-it/

16. Franco, M. E. (2024, April 11). Latine is the new Latinx. *Axios*. https://www.axios.com/2024/04/11/latino-latinx-latine-hispanic-term-explainer

17. Dowd, S. (2022, May 19). Gender-neutral English, dear? We've been using it for centuries! *Babbel Magazine*. https://www.babbel.com/en/magazine/gender-neutral-english

18. 2015 Word of the Year is singular "they." (2016, January 8). *American Dialect Society*. https://americandialect.org/2015-word-of-the-year-is-singular-they

19. Singular "they." (2022, July). *APA Style*. https://apastyle.apa.org/style-grammar-guidelines/grammar/singular-they

CHAPTER 2

1. Hofstede, G., & Hofstede, G. J. (2010). *Cultures and organizations: Software of the mind*. McGraw-Hill.

2. Hofstede and Hofstede (2010).

3. Simons, L., & Zielenziger, M. (1996, March 5). Culture clash dims U.S. future in Asia. *San Jose Mercury News*, pp. A1, A22.

4. McManus, M. R. (2023, August 21). Obscene hand signs and gestures from around the world. *Howstuffworks*. https://people.howstuffworks.com/nonverbal-communication.htm

5. Ting-Toomey, S., & Chung, L. C. (2021). *Understanding intercultural communication*. Oxford University Press.

6. Ting-Toomey and Chung (2021).

7. Pringle, P. (2023). Expecting a direct answer from the Japanese may be "difficult." *Japan Intercultural Consulting*. https://bigthink.com/the-future/artificial-general-intelligence-true-ai/

8. Carufel, R. (2022, March 14). Bad connection: Study finds poor communication costs businesses $1.2 trillion annually. *Agility PR Solutions*. https://www.agilitypr.com/pr-news/public-relations/bad-connection-study-finds-poor-communication-costs-businesses-1-2-trillion-annually/

9. Marriage and couples. (2024). *Gottman Institute*. https://www.gottman.com/about/research/couples/

10. Jaschik, S. (2015, January 20). Well-prepared in their own eyes. *Inside Higher Ed*. https://www.insidehighered.com/news/2015/01/20/study-finds-big-gaps-between-student-and-employer-perceptions; James, A., & Nunamaker, T. (2021, February 1). The communication competency: Exploring student intern and employer communication differences. *National Association of Colleges and Employers*. https://www.naceweb.org/career-readiness/competencies/the-communication-competency-exploring-student-intern-and-employer-communication-differences/

11. Solomon, C. (2016). Trends in global virtual teams. *CultureWizard*. http://cdn.culturewizard.com/PDF/Trends_in_VT_Report_4-17-2016.pdf

12. The cost of bad communication is skyrocketing—what CMOs need to know. (2022, February 24). *Search Engine Land*. https://searchengineland.com/the-cost-of-bad-communication-is-skyrocketing-what-cmos-need-to-know-380456

13. Adler, S. (2023, December 23). Effects of poor communication in healthcare. *HIPAA Journal*. https://www.hipaajournal.com/effects-of-poor-communication-in-healthcare/

14. Dunning, D. (2017, June 14). We are all confident idiots. *Pacific Standard*. https://psmag.com/social-justice/confident-idiots-92793

15. Hayes, L. N. (2018, February 22). The most unusual interview mistakes and biggest body language mishaps, according to annual CareerBuilder survey. *CareerBuilder*. https://press.careerbuilder.com/2018-02-22-The-Most-Unusual-Interview-Mistakes-and-Biggest-Body-Language-Mishaps-According-to-Annual-CareerBuilder-Survey

16. Top 10 unbelievable interview blunders. (2023). *CareerBuilder*. https://www.careerbuilder.ca/jobposter/small-business/article.aspx?articleid=ATL_0174INTERVIEWBLUNDERS

17. Spitzberg, B. H. (2015). Intercultural communication competence. In L. A. Samovar, R. E. Porter, E. R. McDaniel, & C. S. Roy (Eds.), *Intercultural communication: A reader*. Cengage.

18. Shimanoff, S. B. (2009). Rules theory. In S. W. Littlejohn & K. A. Foss (Eds.), *Encyclopedia of communication theory*. Sage.

19. Ting-Toomey, S., & Dorjee, T. (2018). *Communicating across cultures*. Guilford Press.

20. Tipping. (2020, January 19). *Wikitravel*. http://wikitravel.org/en/Tipping

21. Smith, L. (2018, April 5). Why watching cat videos is totally good for you (because, science). *HealthiNation*. https://www.healthination.com/health/cat-videos-health-benefits/

22. Quoted in Bolton, R. (1979). *People skills: How to assert yourself, listen to others, and resolve conflicts*. Simon & Schuster.

23. Derber, C. (1979). *The pursuit of attention: Power and individualism in everyday life*. Oxford University Press.

24. Aune, K. S., Kim, M., & Hu, A. (2000). "Well I've been talking long enough about me. . . . What do you think of my accomplishments?" The relationship between self-construals, narcissism, compulsive talking, and bragging. Paper presented at the meeting of the National Communication Association, Seattle, WA.

25. Vangelisti, A., Knapp, M., & Daly, J. (1990). Conversational narcissism. *Communication Monographs*, 57, 251–274.

26. Derber (1979); Vangelisti et al. (1990, pp. 251–274).

27. Leit, L., Jabovitz, D., & Hazen-Swann, N. (2008). *Conversational narcissism in marriage: Narcissistic attention seeking behaviors in face-to-face interactions: Implications for marital stability and partner mental health*. VDM Verlag.

28. Keltner, D. (2016). *The power paradox*. Penguin Press.

29. Kjerulf, A. (2017, December 6). #1 cause of unhappiness at work: Bad bosses. *HuffPost*. https://www.huffpost.com/entry/1-cause-of-unhappiness-at-work_b_8590416

CHAPTER 3

1. Emerson, M. S. (2023, February 6). 8 tips for better communication skills. *Forbes*. https://www.forbes.com/sites/harvard-division-of-continuing-education/2023/02/06/8-tips-for-better-communication-skills/

2. Schewitz, S. (2023, August 17). How to deal with stalkers. *WikiHow*. https://www.wikihow.com/Deal-With-Stalkers; Wondrak, I., & Hoffman, J. (2007, April/May). A personal obsession: What drives stalkers to pursue their victims? *Scientific American Mind*, pp. 76–81.

3. Lopez, C., & Ward, M. (2020, June 5). 12 things you should never say to your LGBTQ coworkers. *Business Insider*. https://www.businessinsider.com/lgbtq-workers-discrimination-things-not-to-say-2019-9

4. Bernieri, F. J. (2001). Toward a taxonomy of interpersonal sensitivity. In J. A. Hall & F. J. Bernieri (Eds.), *Interpersonal sensitivity: Theory and measurement*. Erlbaum.

5. Cited in Murphy, K. (2019). *You're not listening: What you're missing and why it matters*. Celadon Books.

6. Griffin, E., Ledbetter, A., & Sparks, G. (2019). *A first look at communication theory*. McGraw-Hill.

7. See also Knights, J. (2017). How to develop ethical leaders. *Routledge*. https://www.routledge.com/posts/9951

8. Triandis, H. C. (2009). Ecological determinants of cultural variations. In R. S. Wyer, C. Chiu, Y. Hong, & D. Cohen (Eds.), *Understanding culture: Theory, research and applications*. Psychology Press.

9. Harrison, L. E. (2000). Introduction. In L. E. Harrison & S. P. Huntington (Eds.), *Culture matters: How values shape human progress*. Basic Books.

CHAPTER 4

1. Swann, W. B., Rentfrow, P. J., & Gosling, S. D. (2003). The precarious couple effect: Verbally inhibited men + critical, disinhibited women = bad chemistry. *Journal of Personality and Social Psychology*, 85, 1095–1106.

2. Hung, K.-P., & Lin, C.-K. (2013). More communication is not always better? The interplay between effective communication and interpersonal conflict in influencing satisfaction. *Industrial Marketing Management*, 42, 1223–1232.

3. Tumlin, G. (2013, September 9). 5 reasons more communication isn't better. *Government Executive*. https://www.govexec.com/management/2013/09/5-reasons-more-communication-isnt-better/70092/

4. Global study: 70% of business leaders would prefer a robot to make their decisions. (2023, April 19). *Oracle*. https://www.prnewswire.com/news-releases/global-study-70-of-business-leaders-would-prefer-a-robot-to-make-their-decisions-301799591.html

5. The path to productivity, performance, and profit: 2023 state of business communication. (2023). *Grammarly Business*. https://go.grammarly.com/business-communication-report

6. Steele, C. (2022, November 23). Space wars: 80s CRAY-2 supercomputer vs. modern-day iPhone. *PCMag*. https://www.pcmag.com/news/space-wars-the-cray-2-supercomputer-vs-the-iphone-12

7. MacKay, J. (2018, July 10). Communication overload: Research shows most workers can't go 6 minutes without checking email or IM. *Medium*. https://medium.com/swlh/communication-overload-research-shows-most-workers-cant-go-6-minutes-without-checking-email-or-im-8ef4392a7159

8. Rosen, C. C., Simon, L. S., & Gajendran, R. S., Johnson, R. E., Lee, H. W., & Lin, S.-H. (2019). Boxed in by your inbox: Implications of daily e-mail demands for managers' leadership behaviors. *Journal of Applied Psychology, 104*, 19–33. https://doi.org/10.1037/apl0000343

9. Spira, J. B. (2011). *Overload: How too much information is hazardous to your organization*. Wiley.

10. Rock, D. (2009). *Your brain at work*. HarperCollins.

11. Quoted by Gregoire, C. (2013, December 6). How technology speeds up time (and how to slow it down again). *HuffPost*. http://www.huffingtonpost.com/2013/12/06/technology-time-perception_n_4378010.html

12. Global study: 70% of business leaders would prefer a robot to make their decisions.

13. Baror, S., & Bar, M. (2016). Associative activation and its relation to exploration and exploitation in the brain. *Psychological Science, 27*, 776–789. https://doi.org/10.1177%2F0956797616634487

14. Baer, D. (2016, June 20). Unloaded minds are the most creative. *The Cut*. https://www.thecut.com/2016/06/unloaded-minds-are-the-most-creative.html

15. Franganillo, J. (2017, May). Information overload, why it matters and how to combat it. *Interaction Design Foundation*. https://www.interaction-design.org/literature/article/information-overload-why-it-matters-and-how-to-combat-it; Shin, L. (2014, November 14). 10 steps to conquering information overload. *Forbes*. https://www.forbes.com/sites/laurashin/2014/11/14/10-steps-to-conquering-information-overload/; Silver, N. (2012). *The*

signal and the noise: Why so many predictions fail—but some don't. Penguin Press.

16. Burkus, D. (2016, May 16). Why your inbox is your enemy. *Inc.* https://www.inc.com/david-burkus/youre-kidding-yourself-email-is-actually-killing-your-productivity.html

17. Sma, S., Schrift, R. Y., & Zauberman, G. (2018). The illusion of multitasking and its positive effect on performance. *Psychological Science*, 29, 1942–1955.

18. Poljac, E., Kiesel, A., Koch, I., & Muller, H. (2018). New perspectives on human multitasking. *Psychological Research*,82, 1–3. https://doi.org/10.1007/s00426-018-0970-2; Schmidt, S. J.(2020). Distracted learning: Big problem and golden opportunity. *Journal ofFood Science Education*, 19, 278–291. https://onlinelibrary.wiley.com/doi/pdf/10.1111/1541-4329.12206

19. Interview: Clifford Nass. (2010, February 2). *PBS.* https://www.pbs.org/wgbh/pages/frontline/digitalnation/interviews/nass.html

CHAPTER 5

1. Baker, G. (2015, July 31). Five top causes of "business communication problems." *AdvanceConsulting.* https://www.advanceconsulting.com/blog/five-top-causes-of-business-communication-problems/

2. Weir, K. (2018). What makes teams work? *Monitor.* https://www.apa.org/monitor/2018/09/cover-teams

3. Carufel, R. (2022, March 14). Bad connection: Study finds poor communication costs businesses $1.2 trillion annually. *Agility PR Solutions.* https://www.agilitypr.com/pr-news/public-relations/bad-connection-study-finds-poor-communication-costs-businesses-1-2-trillion-annually/. See also Brodnitz, D. (2024, February 8). The most in-demand skills for 2024. *LinkedIn.* https://www.linkedin.com/business/talent/blog/talent-strategy/linkedin-most-in-demand-hard-and-soft-skills

4. Corporate recruiters survey report 2017. (2017). *Graduate Management Admission Council.* file:///C:/Users/darot/Downloads/2017-gmac-corporate-recruiters-web-release.pdf

5. Barrett, J. (2018, April 19). The U.S. is facing a critical skills shortage, reskilling can be part of the solution. *LinkedIn.* https://blog.linkedin.com/2018/april/19/the-u-s-is-facing-a-critical-skills-shortage-reskilling-can-be-part-of-the-solution. See also Bauer-Wolf, J. (2019, January 17). Survey: Employers want "soft skills" from graduates. *Inside Higher Education.* https://www.insidehighered.com/quicktakes/2019/01/17/survey-employers-want-soft-skills-graduates

6. 2018 student survey report. (2019). *National Association of Colleges and Employers*. https://www.naceweb.org/store/2018/2018-nace-student-survey-report/

7. Morreale, S. P., Broeckelman-Post, M. A., Anderson, L. B., Ledford, V. A., & Westwick, J. N. (2023, March 3). The importance, significance, and relevance of communication: A fourth study of the criticality of the discipline's content and pedagogy. *Communication Education*. https://www.tandfonline.com/doi/full/10.1080/03634523.2023.2178663

8. Warzel, C., & Petersen, A. H. (2021). *Out of office*. Alfred A. Knopf.

CHAPTER 6

1. Bryson, B. (1990). *The mother tongue: English and how it got that way*. Avon Books.

2. Rothwell, J. D. (1982). *Telling it like it isn't: Language misuse and malpractice*. Prentice Hall.

3. Koyfman, S. (2020, June 22). How do you say "salty" in multiple languages? *Babbel*. https://www.babbel.com/en/magazine/best-curse-words-in-other-languages

4. Bryson (1990).

5. Norquist, R. (2020, April 5). The basic elements of the communication process. *ThoughtCo*. https://www.thoughtco.com/what-is-communication-process-1689767

6. Boudreau, J. (2007, August 12). Beijing brushes up on its English skills. *San Jose Mercury News*, p. 17A.

7. Liao, A. (2017, May). What's the most complicated word in English? *Bookstr*. https://www.bookstr.com/most-complicated-word-english

CHAPTER 7

1. Sacks, O. (1990). *Seeing voices: A journey into the world of the deaf*. Vintage Books.

2. Pinker, S. (2011). The language instinct. *Brilliance Audio*.

3. How many languages are there in the world? 7,168 languages are in use today. (2022). *Ethnologue*. https://www.ethnologue.com/insights/how-many-languages/

4. Quadir, S. (2020, November). Speech sounds in world languages. *City University of London*. https://www.city.ac.uk/news-and-events/news/2020/02/speech-sounds-in-the-worlds

5. Crystal, D. (2005). *How language works: How babies babble, words change meaning, and languages live or die*. Overlook Press.

6. Ager, S. (2023). Czech tongue twisters. *Omniglot*. https://omniglot .com/language/tonguetwisters/czech.htm

7. Crystal, D. (1997). *The Cambridge encyclopedia of language*. Cambridge University Press.

8. Features of language. (2021, June 26). *LibreTexts*. https://socialsci .libretexts.org/Bookshelves/Anthropology/Cultural_Anthropology/Cultural _Anthropology_(Wikibook)/4%3A_Communication_and_Language/ 4.4%3A_Features_of_Language

9. Number of words in the English language. (2022, November 14). *Global Language Monitor*. https://languagemonitor.com/category/number-of -words-in-english/new-english-words-per-day/

10. Oakley, A. (2016), March 24). Amazing obsolete words in the English dictionary we should bring back. *Express Writers*. https://expresswriters.com /amazing-obsolete-words-in-the-english-dictionary/

11. Pinker (2011).

12. Adger, D. (2019, September 17). This simple structure unites all human languages. *Nautilus*. https://nautil.us/this-simple-structure-unites-all -human-languages-237546/

13. Features of language.

14. DeVito, J. (1970). *The psychology of speech and language: An introduction to psycholinguistics*. Random House.

15. Sacks (1990). See also Kyuseva, M. (2021, May 12). Sign language mythbusters. *Morph*. https://morph.surrey.ac.uk/index.php/2021/05/12/sign -language-mythbusters/

16. Crystal (2005).

17. A guide to different types of sign language. (2023, February). *Interpret Cloud*. https://www.interpretcloud.com/blog/a-guide-to-different-types -of-sign-language/

18. Unzueta, V. G. (2021, April 15). Black American Sign Language (BASL). *The Project of the History of Black Writing*. https://projecthbw.ku .edu/uncategorized/black-american-sign-language-basl/

19. American Sign Language. (2021, October 29). *National Institute on Deafness and Other Communication Disorders*. https://www.nidcd.nih.gov/ health/american-sign-language

20. An introduction to ASL Grammar Rules. (2022, October 5). *Proofed*. https://proofed.com/writing-tips/an-introduction-to-asl-grammar-rules/

21. Abdulghafor, R., Turaev, S., and Ali, M. A. H. (2022, July). Body language analysis in healthcare: An overview. *Healthcare* (Basel), *10*(7), Article 1251. https://www.ncbi.nlm.nih.gov/pmc/articles/PMC9325107/

22. Patterson, M. L., Fridlund, A. J., & Crivelli, C. (2023). Four misconceptions about nonverbal communication. *Perspectives on Psychological Science*. https://journals.sagepub.com/doi/full/10.1177/17456916221148142

23. Patterson et al. (2023).

24. Bond, C. F., & DePaulo, B. M. (2006). Accuracy of deception judgments. *Personality and Social Psychology, 10,* 214–234; Porter, S., & ten Brinke, L. (2010). Truth about lies: What works in detecting high-stakes deception? *Legal and Criminological Psychology, 15,* 57–76.

25. Ekman, P. (2024, July 25). Deception detection. *Paul Ekman Group.* https://www.paulekman.com/deception/deception-detection/

26. Patterson et al. (2023).

CHAPTER 8

1. Michail, J. (2020, August 24). Strong nonverbal skills matter now more than ever in this "new normal." *Forbes.* https://www.forbes.com/sites/forbescoachescouncil/2020/08/24/strong-nonverbal-skills-matter-now-more-than-ever-in-this-new-normal/?sh=269e5ae65c61

2. Heathfield, S. M.(2022, September 13). How to understand your coworkers' nonverbal communication.*The Balance.* https://www.thebalancemoney.com/tips-for-understanding-nonverbal-communication-1918459

3. Brodie, I. (2021). Debunking the myths of non-verbal communication. *Ianbrodie.com.* https://www.ianbrodie.com/debunking-the-myths-of-non-verbal-communication/

4. Uebergang, J. (2020). The greatest 15 myths of communication. *Tower of Power.* https://www.towerofpower.com.au/the-greatest-15-myths-of-communication

5. See Lapakko, D.(2007). Communication is 93% nonverbal: An urban legend proliferates. *Communicationand Theater Association of Minnesota Journal, 34,* 7–19. See also Konstantinova, M., & Astakhova, K. (2018, November 16). Experts say . . . Is communication really only 7% verbal? Truth vs. marketing. *MediumMarketing.* https://medium.com/@neurodatalab/experts-say-is-communication-really-only-7-verbal-truth-vs-marketing-9a8e7428fd0f

6. Quoted by Lovett, M. (2016, August 14). Exploring the Mehrabian myth. *Storytelling with Impact.* https://www.storytellingwithimpact.com/exploring-the-mehrabian-myth/

7. Rothwell, J. D. (1982). *Telling it like it isn't: Language misuse and malpractice.* Prentice Hall. See also Rothwell, J. D. (2016). *In the company*

of others: An introduction to communication. Oxford University Press; and Rothwell, J. D. (2023). *Practically speaking*. Oxford University Press.

8. Fairhurst, G. (2011). *The power of framing: Creating the language of leadership*. Jossey-Bass. See also Meeks, L. (2020). Defining the enemy: How Donald Trump frames the news media. *Journal of Mass Communication Quarterly*. https://doi.org/10.1177/1077699019857676

9. Fairhurst, G. T., & Sarr, R. A. (1996). *The art of framing: Managing the language of leadership*. Jossey-Bass.

10. Perera, A, (2023, September 7). Framing effect in psychology. *Simply Psychology*. https://www.simplypsychology.org/framing-effect.html#Examples

11. Feinberg, M., & Willer, R. (2015). From gulf to bridge: When do moral arguments facilitate political influence? *Personality and Social Psychology*, *41*, 1665–1681.

12. Thibodeau, P. H., & Boroditsky, L. (2011). Metaphors we think with: The role of metaphor in reasoning. *PLOS ONE*. https://journals.plos.org/plosone/article?id=10.1371/journal.pone.0016782

13. Kahan, D. M., Hoffman, D. A., Braman, D., Evans, D., & Rachlinski, J. J. (2012). "They saw a protest": Cognitive illiberalism and the speech-conduct distinction. *Stanford Law Review*, *64*, 851–906.

14. Dube, S. R., Li, E.T., Fiorini, G., et al. (2023, October). Childhood verbal abuse as a child maltreatment subtype: A systematic review of the current evidence. *Science Digest*. https://www.sciencedirect.com/science/article/abs/pii/S0145213423003824

15. Teicher, M. H., Samson, J. A., Sheu, Y.-S., Polcari, A., & McGreenery, C. E. (2010). Hurtful words: Association of exposure to peer verbal abuse with elevated psychiatric symptom scores and corpus callosum abnormalities. *American Journal of Psychiatry*, *167*, 1464–1471.

16. Putnam, F. W. (2010). Beyond sticks and stones. *American Journal of Psychiatry*, *167*, 1422–1424. See also Quinn, J. M., & Wood, W. (2004). Forewarnings of influence appeals: Inducing resistance and acceptance. In E. S. Knowles & J. A. Linn (Eds.), *Resistance and persuasion*. Erlbaum.

17. Brewer, C. S., Kovner, C. T., Obcidat, R. F., & Budin, W. C. (2013). Positive work environments of early-career registered nurses and the correlation with physician verbal abuse.*Nursing Outlook*, *61*, 408–416.

18. Quoted by Robbins, A. (2015). *Unlimited power: The new science of personal achievement*. Simon & Schuster Paperbacks.

19. Brewer et al. (2013, 408–416); Grenny, J. (2009). Crucial conversations: The most potent force for eliminating disruptive behavior. *Physician Executive Journal*, *35*, 30–33.

20. Maxfield, D., Grenny, J., McMillan, R., Patterson, K., & Switzler, A. (2005). Silence kills: The seven crucial conversations in healthcare.

VitalSmarts. http://www.silencekills.com/UPDL/SilenceKillsExecSummary .pdf. See also Pavek, C. H., & Steege, L. M. (2020, August 19). Workplace verbal abuse, nurse-reported quality of care, and patient safety outcomes among early-career hospital nurses. *Journal of Nursing Management*. https://psnet.ahrq.gov/issue/workplace-verbal-abuse-nurse-reported-quality-care -and-patient-safety-outcomes-among-early

21. Pollack, R. J. (2022, March 23). AHA urges DOJ to protect health care workers from workplace violence. *American Hospital Association*. https://www.aha.org/lettercomment/2022-03-24-aha-urges-doj-protect-health-care -workers-workplace-violence

22. Eye contact—a declining communications tool? (2013, June 27). *Quantified*. https://www.quantified.ai/blog/eye-contact-a-declining-communications-tool/

23. Kraus, M. W., & Keltner, D. (2009, January 1). Signs of socioeconomic status: A thin-slicing approach. *Psychological Science*. https://journals.sagepub.com/doi/abs/10.1111/j.1467-9280.2008.02251.x

24. Murcott, M. (2016). The customer rage study. *Dialog Direct*. https://epicconnections.com/wp-content/uploads/2016/04/DialogDirect_CustRage _Guide_v5_0.pdf

25. Page, S. (2023, March 8). A GOP war on "woke"? Most Americans view the term as a positive, USA TODAY/Ipsos poll finds. *USA Today*. https://www.usatoday.com/story/news/politics/2023/03/08/gop-war-woke -most-americans-see-term-positive-ipsos-poll/11417394002/

26. Serico, C. (2015, February 22). Neil Patrick Harris hosts the Oscars: Catch up on all his best lines. *Today Pop Culture*. http://www.today .com/popculture/neil-patrick-harris-hosts-oscars-all-his-best-lines-academy -2D80504883

27. Thompson, J. (2011, September 30). Is nonverbal communication a numbers game? *Psychology Today*. https://www.psychologytoday.com/us/ blog/beyond-words/201109/is-nonverbal-communication-numbers-game

28. Manolaki, A. (2016, August 30). Translating body language signs in different cultures. *Terminology Coordination: European Parliament*. http:// termcoord.eu/2016/08/translating-body-language-signs-in-different-cultures/

CHAPTER 9

1. Weir, K. (2023, March 1). Ageism is one of the last socially acceptable prejudices. *Monitor on Psychology*. https://www.apa.org/monitor/2023/03/ cover-new-concept-of-aging

2. Samson, C. (2023, May 8). 10 anti-Asian stereotypes that need to be dumped NOW. *Center for Racial Healing*. https://www.centerforracial healing.org/post/10-anti-asian-stereotypes-that-need-to-be-dumped-now

3. Shpancer, N. (2018, September 20). Stereotype accuracy: A displeasing truth. *Psychology Today*. https://www.psychologytoday.com/us/blog/insight-therapy/201809/stereotype-accuracy-displeasing-truth

4. Lee, Y.-T., Jussim, L. J., & McCauley, C. R. (1995). *Stereotype accuracy: Toward appreciating group differences*. American Psychological Association; Shpancer (2018).

5. Peterson, E. (2017, Fall). Why not all stereotypes are bad. *THINK: Case Western Reserve University*. https://case.edu/think/fall2017/stereotypes.html

6. Shpancer (2018).

7. Sevillano, V., & Fiske, S. T. (2023, June). Animals are diverse: Distinct forms of animalized dehumanization. *Current Opinion in Behavioral Sciences*. https://www.sciencedirect.com/science/article/pii/S2352154623000190. See also Strauss, B. (2018, January 2). 12 animal stereotypes and the truth behind them. *ThoughtCo*. https://www.thoughtco.com/animal-stereotypes-4136106

8. Jonas, K. J., & Sassenberg, K. (2006). Knowing how to react: Automatic response priming from social categories. *Journal of Personality and Social Psychology*, 90, 709–721.

9. Lombrozo, T. (2015, July 20). The negative in positive stereotypes. *NPR*. https://www.npr.org/sections/13.7/2015/07/20/424640508/the-negative-in-positive-stereotypes

10. Correll, J., Park, B., Judd, C. M., & Wittenbrink, B. (2002). The police officer's dilemma: Using ethnicity to disambiguate potentially threatening individuals. *Journal of Personality and Social Psychology*, 83, 1314–1329.

11. Bunn, C. (2022, March 3). Report: Black people are still killed by police at a higher rate than other groups. *NBC News*. https://www.nbcnews.com/news/nbcblk/report-black-people-are-still-killed-police-higher-rate-groups-rcna17169

12. McNatt, D. B. (2000). Ancient Pygmalion joins contemporary management: A meta-analysis of the result. *Journal of Applied Psychology*, 85, 314–322.

13. Snyder, M. (2001). Self-fulfilling stereotypes.In A. Branaman (Ed.), *Self and society: Blackwell readers in sociology*. Blackwell.

14. Pinel, E. C. (1999). Stigma consciousness: The psychological legacy of social stereotypes. *Journal of Personality and Social Psychology*, 76, 114–128.

15. Wick, J. (2015). Stereotyping in 170 milliseconds. *Longreads*. https://longreads.com/2015/04/29/stereotyping-in-170-milliseconds/

16. Czopp, A. M., Monteith, M. J., & Mark, A. Y. (2006). Standing up for a change: Reducing bias through interpersonal confrontation. *Journal of Personality and Social Psychology*, 90, 784–803.

17. Hodson, G. (2011). Do ideologically intolerant people benefit from intergroup contact? *Current Directions in Psychological Science*, 20, 154–159. See also Hopper, E. (2019, October 26). What is the contact hypothesis in psychology? *ThoughtCo*. https://www.thoughtco.com/contact-hypothesis-4772161

18. Pettigrew, T. F., & Tropp, L. R. (2006). A meta-analytic test of intergroup contact theory. *Journal of Personality and Social Psychology*, 90, 751–783.

19. McLeod, S. (2023, June 15). Allport's intergroup contact hypothesis: Its history and influence. *SimplyPsychology*. https://www.simplypsychology.org/contact-hypothesis.html

20. McLeod (2023).

21. Aging and disability: Beyond stereotypes to inclusion: Proceedings of a workshop. (2018). *National Center for Biotechnical Information*. https://www.ncbi.nlm.nih.gov/books/NBK513022/

CHAPTER 10

1. Mirivel, J. C., & Lyon, A. (2023). *Positive communication for leaders: Proven strategies for inspiring unity and effecting change*. Rowman & Littlefield.

2. Mirivel and Lyon (2023).

3. Borresen, K. (2023, July 21). You should probably start paying more attention to "bids" in your relationship. *HuffPost*. https://www.huffpost.com/entry/pay-attention-bids-connection-relationship_l_64b970d7e4b0dcb4cab7ecab

4. Ledbetter, A. M., & Keating, A. T. (2015). Maintaining Facebook friendships: Everyday talk as a mediator of threats to closeness. *Western Journal of Communication*, 79, 197–217.

5. Ury, L. (2024, September 19). Want to improve your relationship? Start paying more attention to bids. *Gottman Institute*. https://www.gottman.com/blog/want-to-improve-your-relationship-start-paying-more-attention-to-bids/

6. Gottman, J. M., & DeClaire, J. (2001). *The relationship cure: A five-step guide for building better connections with family, friends, and lovers*. Crown Books.

7. Gottman and DeClaire (2001).

8. Brittle, Z. (2023). Turn towards instead of away. *Gottman Institute*. https://www.gottman.com/blog/turn-toward-instead-of-away/; Smith, E. E. (2014, June 12). Masters of love. *The Atlantic*. http://www.theatlantic.com/health/archive/2014/06/happily-ever-after/372573/

9. Ury (2024).

CHAPTER 11

1. Moore, C. (2021, April 26). What is the negativity bias and how can it be overcome? *Positive Psychology*. https://positivepsychology.com/3-steps-negativity-bias/

2. Hanson, R. (2016, October 26). Confronting the negativity bias. *Rickhanson.net*. http://www.rickhanson.net/how-your-brain-makes-you-easily-intimidated/

3. Hanson (2016).

4. Tierney, J., & Baumeister, R. F. (2020). *The power of bad: How the negativity effect rules us and how we can rule it*. Penguin Press.

5. Forbes Coaches Council. (2021, April 23). Balancing criticism and praise: 13 tips for company leaders. *Forbes*. https://www.forbes.com/sites/forbescoachescouncil/2021/04/23/balancing-criticism-and-praise-13-tips-for-company-leaders/

6. Quoted by Goleman, D. (2013). *Focus: The hidden driver of excellence*. HarperCollins.

7. Ko, V. (2013, April 14). Can you cope with criticism at work? *CNN*. http://www.cnn.com/2013/04/14/business/criticism-praise-feedback-work-life/index.html

8. Tierney and Baumeister (2020).

9. Lybormirsky, S., King, L., & Diener, E. (2005). The benefits of frequent positive affect: Does happiness lead to success? *Psychological Bulletin, 131*, 803–855.

10. Fredrickson, B. L. (2010). *Positivity: Top-notch research reveals the 3-to-1 ratio that will change your life*. Three Rivers Press.

11. Tierney and Baumeister (2020).

12. Benson, K. (2023). The anger iceberg. *Gottman Institute*. https://www.gottman.com/blog/the-anger-iceberg/

13. Rusnak, K. (2023). The magic ratio: The key to relationship satisfaction. *Gottman Institute*. https://www.gottman.com/blog/the-magic-ratio-the-key-to-relationship-satisfaction/

14. Grenny, J. (2019, June 17). How to be resilient in the face of harsh criticism. *Harvard Business Review*. https://hbr.org/2019/06/how-to-be-resilient-in-the-face-of-harsh-criticism

15. Snyder, K. (2014, August 26). The abrasiveness trap: High-achieving men and women are described differently in reviews. *Fortune*. https://fortune.com/2014/08/26/performance-review-gender-bias/

16. Stosny, S. (2014, April 18). What's wrong with criticism. *Psychology Today*. https://www.psychologytoday.com/blog/anger-in-the-age-entitlement/201404/whats-wrong-criticism

17. Stosny (2014).

18. Ryan, N. (2020, February 19). The four horsemen: Signs your relationship is in trouble. *Sacwellness*. https://sacwellness.com/the-four-horsemen-signs-your-relationship-is-in-trouble/

19. Nink, M., & Robinson, J. (2021, February 9). Add team praise to your employee recognition toolkit. *Workplace*. https://www.gallup.com/workplace/329351/add-team-praise-employee-recognition-toolkit.aspx

20. Nass, C. (2010). The man who lied to his laptop: What machines teach us about human relationships. *Your Coach in a Box*. [CD]. Penguin Press.

21. Hornsey, M. J., Robson, E., Smith, J., Esposo, S., & Sutton, R. M. (2008). Sugaring the pill: Assessing rhetorical strategies designed to minimize defensive reactions to group criticism. *Human Communication Research, 34*, 70–98.

22. Ward, M., Akhtar, A., & Lebowitz, S. (2020, March 16). 26 signs you have a terrible boss, and how to stop them from crushing your happiness. *Insider*. https://www.businessinsider.com/signs-you-have-a-bad-boss-2016-2-4

23. Greengross, G., & Miller, G. F. (2008). Dissing oneself versus dissing rivals: Effects of status, personality, and sex on the short-term and long-term attractiveness of self-deprecating and other-deprecating humor. *Evolutionary Psychology Journal, 6*, 393–408.

24. Elsesser, K. (2019, March 15). Women can use humor at work, but they should follow this advice. *Forbes*. https://www.forbes.com/sites/kimelsesser/2019/03/15/women-can-use-humor-at-work-but-they-should-follow-this-advice/

25. Porath, C. (2016). *Mastering civility: A manifesto for the workplace*. Grand Central Publishing.

26. Quoted by Ross, M. (2017, April 9). Civility suits the workplace. *San Jose Mercury News*, pp. D1, D8.

27. Antoci, A., Boneli, L., Paglieri, F., Reggiani, T. G., & Sabatini, F. (2018). Civility and trust in social media. *IZA Institute of Labor Economics*. http://ftp.iza.org/dp11290.pdf

CHAPTER 13

1. Jacob, A., & Jacob, A. (2023). Conflict is a normal and natural part of your "happily ever after." *Gottman Institute*. https://www.gottman.com/blog/conflict-normal-natural-part-happily-ever/

2. Gottman couples & marital therapy. (2015). *Couples Training Institute*. https://couplestraininginstitute.com/gottman-couples-and-marital-therapy/

3. Tafvelin, S., Keisu, B.-I., & Kvist, E. (2020). The prevalence and consequences of intragroup conflicts for employee well-being in women-dominated work. *Human Services Organizations: Management, Leadership & Governance*. https://www.tandfonline.com/doi/full/10.1080/23303131.2019.1661321

4. Kerwin, S., Doherty, A., & Harman, A. (2011). "It's not conflict, it's differences of opinion": An in-depth examination of conflict in nonprofit boards. *Small Group Research, 42,* 562–594.

5. Conroy, J. (2023, May 18). Positive conflict in the workplace. *Exude*. https://www.exudeinc.com/blog/positive-conflict-in-the-workplace/; Omisore, B. O., & Abiodun, A. R. (2014). Organizational conflicts: Causes, effects and remedies. *International Journal of Academic Research in Economics and Management Sciences*. https://pdfs.semanticscholar.org/dc47/343acf285d3c6e7af9d5bb935981ac251c02.pdf

6. Fostering constructive conflict in team negotiation. (2020, December 3). *Program on Negotiation, Harvard Law School*. https://www.pon.harvard.edu/daily/conflict-resolution/fostering-constructive-conflict-in-teams-nb/

7. Wilmot, W., & Hocker, J. (2022). *Interpersonal conflict*. McGraw-Hill.

8. Donohue, W. A., & Kolt, R. (1992). *Managing interpersonal conflict*. Sage.

9. Jacobs, J., & Harrison, C. (2019, April 9). Doctor dragged off United Airlines flight after watching viral video of himself: "I just cried." *ABC News*. https://abcnews.go.com/US/doctor-dragged-off-united-airlines-flight-watching-viral/story?id=62250271

10. Wilmot and Hocker (2022).

11. Shonk, K. (2023, March 6). Conflict styles and bargaining styles. *Program on Negotiation, Harvard Law School*. https://www.pon.harvard.edu/daily/conflict-resolution/conflict-styles-and-bargaining-styles/; Kilmann, R. H. (2023). How to use a conflict mode most effectively. *Kilmann Diagnostics*. https://kilmanndiagnostics.com/how-to-use-a-conflict-mode/

12. Shapiro, D. (2017). *Negotiating the nonnegotiable: How to resolve your most emotionally charged conflicts*. Penguin Press.

13. Dubrin, A. J. (2019). *Leadership: Research findings, practice, and skills*. Cengage.

14. Johnson, S. (2023, February 28). What is crowdfunding? *Business News Daily*. https://www.businessnewsdaily.com/4134-what-is-crowdfunding.htm

15. Shonk (2023).

16. Cohen, A. (2020, November 18). How to have difficult conversations. *Psyche*. https://psyche.co/guides/use-mediation-techniques-to-overcome-the-muck-of-blame-and-anger

17. Elgoibar, P., Euweman, M., & Munduate, L. (2017). Conflict management. *Oxford Research Encyclopedia*. https://oxfordre.com/psychology/view/10.1093/acrefore/9780190236557.001.0001/acrefore-9780190236557-e-5

18. Fulwiler, M. (2023). Managing conflict: Solvable vs. perpetual problems. *Gottman Institute*. https://www.gottman.com/blog/managing-conflict-solvable-vs-perpetual-problems

19. Mahdav, A. (2021, July). The most surprisingly contentious subject? Toilet roll orientation. *The Guardian*. https://www.theguardian.com/commentisfree/2021/jul/14/most-surprisingly-contentious-subject-toilet-roll-orientation

20. Elgoibar et al. (2017).

21. Wilmot and Hocker (2022).

22. Brehm, J. (1972). *Responses to loss of freedom: A theory of psychological resistance*. General Learning Press.

23. Moore, S. (2019). Reactance theory & employee performance. *Chron*. https://smallbusiness.chron.com/reactance-theory-employee-performance-34456.html

24. Young, D. G., Rasheed, H., Bleakley, A., & Langbaum, J. B. (2022, April). The politics of mask-wearing: Political preferences, reactance, and conflict aversion during COVID. *Social Science & Medicine*. https://www.sciencedirect.com/science/article/pii/S0277953622001423

25. Ruback, B. R., & Jweng, D. (2006). Territorial defense in parking lots: Retaliation against waiting drivers. *Journal of Applied Social Psychology*, *27*, 821–834. https://doi.org/10.1111/j.1559-1816.1997.tb00661.x

26. Howell, S. E. (2014). Conflict management: A literature review and study. *Radiology Management*. http://www.ahra.org/AM/Downloads/OI/qc/RM365_p14-23_Features.pdf

27. Dubrin (2019); Shonk, K. (2021, October 25). Conflict-managing styles: Pitfalls and best practices. *Program on Negotiation, Harvard Law School*. https://www.pon.harvard.edu/daily/conflict-resolution/conflict-management-styles-pitfalls-and-best-practices/

28. Evans, C. R., & Dion, K. L. (2012). Group cohesion and performance: A meta-analysis. *Small Group Research*, *43*, 690–701. https://doi.org/10.1177%2F1046496412468074

29. Prieto-Remon, T. C., Cobo-Benita, J. R., Ortiz-Marcos, I., & Uruburu, A. (2015). Conflict resolution to project performance. *ResearchGate*. https://www.researchgate.net/publication/282556551_Conflict_Resolution_to_Project_Performance

30. Elgoibar et al. (2017); Somech, A., Desivilya, H. S., & Lidogoster, H. (2008). Team conflict management and team effectiveness: The effects of task interdependence and team identification. *Journal of Organizational Behavior*, *30*, 359–378.

31. "103 Best Max Lucado Quotes." (2022). *Kidadl*. https://kidadl.com/quotes/best-max-lucado-quotes-from-the-american-author-and-pastor

32. Thomas, K. W., & Thomas, G. F. (2008). Conflict styles of men and women at six organizational levels. *International Journal of Conflict Management*, *14*, 1–38.

33. Dildar, S., & Amjad, N. (2017). Gender differences in conflict resolution styles (CRS) in different roles: A systematic review. *Pakistan Journal of Social and Clinical Psychology*, *15*, 37–41. https://gcu.edu.pk/wp-content/uploads/2020/04/pjscp20172-6.pdf

34. Rahim, M. A., & Katz, J. P. (2019). Forty years of conflict: The effects of gender and generation on conflict-management strategies. *International Journal of Conflict Management*, *31*, 1–16. https://doi.org/10.1108/IJCMA-03-2019-0045

35. Felps, W., Mitchell, T. R., & Byington, E. (2006). How, when, and why bad apples spoil the barrel: Negative group members and dysfunctional groups. *Research in Organizational Behavior*, *27*, 175–222.

36. Housman, M., & Minor, D. (2015). Toxic workers. *Harvard Business School*. Working paper 16-047.

CHAPTER 14

1. Control anger before it controls you. (2022, August 9). *American Psychological Association*. https://www.apa.org/topics/anger/control

2. Hammer, L. B., Lee, J. D., Mohr, C. D., & Allen, S. J. (2021). Anger and the role of supervisors at work. *APA PsycNet*. https://psycnet.apa.org/record/2021-63486-006

3. Brogaard, B. (2020, December 29). Anger in your relationships. *Psychology Today*. https://www.psychologytoday.com/us/blog/the-mysteries-love/202012/6-tips-how-manage-anger-in-your-relationships

4. Kjaervik, S., & Bushman, B. J. (2024, April). A meta-analytic review of anger management activities that increase or decrease arousal: What fuels

or douses rage? *Clinical Psychology Review*. https://www.sciencedirect.com/science/article/pii/S0272735824000357

5. Hodge, K. (2023, June 22). Do I need treatment for my anger problem? Finding peace within. *Mental Health Center*. https://www.mentalhealthcenter.org/treatment-for-my-anger-problem/

6. Yip, J. A., & Schweitzer, M. E. (2019). Losing your temper and your perspective: Anger reduces perspective-taking. *Organizational Behavior and Human Decision Processes*.https://www.sciencedirect.com/science/article/abs/pii/S0749597816308172

7. Boland, M. (2021, May 17). Emotional minutes: Venting and the myths of catharsis. *Emotional Minutes*. https://mattbphd.com/emotional-minutes-18-emotional-venting-and-the-myths-of-catharsis/

8. Trepany, C. (2024, May 8). Women are paying big money to scream, smash sticks in the woods. It's called a rage ritual. *USA Today*. https://www.usatoday.com/story/life/health-wellness/2024/05/08/rage-rituals-women-screaming-woods-why/73595511007/

9. Salters-Pedneault, K. (2022, March 25). Is venting your anger a good idea? *Verywellmind*. https://www.verywellmind.com/how-you-vent-anger-may-not-be-good-for-bpd-425393; Kjaervik and Bushman (2024).

10. Quoted by Mclendon, R. (2024, April). Venting doesn't reduce anger, but something else does, study finds. *ScienceAlert*. https://www.sciencealert.com/venting-doesnt-reduce-anger-but-something-else-does-study-finds

11. Yip and Schweitzer (2019).

12. Gottman, J. M., & Gottman, J. S. (2006). *10 lessons to transform your marriage*. Crown.

13. Hyder, S. (2023). How to handle anger in your relationships. *Gottman Institute*. https://www.gottman.com/blog/handle-anger-relationship/

14. Navarra, R. (2023). The dark side of anger: What every couple should know. *Gottman Institute*. https://www.gottman.com/blog/the-dark-side-of-anger-what-every-couple-should-know/

15. McClendon, R. (2024, November 21). Venting doesn't reduce anger, but something else does, study shows. *ScienceAlert*. https://www.sciencealert.com/venting-doesnt-reduce-anger-but-something-else-does-study-shows

CHAPTER 15

1. Meetings: The good, the bad, and the ugly. (2015, September 16). *Wharton*. http://knowledge.wharton.upenn.edu/article/meetings-the-good-the-bad-and-the-ugly

2. Haden, J. (2017, July 10). Why 99 percent of all meetings are a complete waste of money and time. *Inc.* https://www.inc.com/jeff-haden/why-99-percent-of-all-meetings-are-a-complete-wast.html

3. Doodle. (2019). The state of meetings report. *Norma.* https://meeting-report.com/; Levitt, J. (2013) Seven symptoms of bad meetings and what you can do about them. *LCE.* https://www.lce.com/Seven-Symptoms-of-Bad-Meetings-and-What-You-Can-Do-About-Them-1408.html

4. Supiano, B. (2020, April 23). Why is Zoom so exhausting? *The Chronicle of Higher Education.* https://www.chronicle.com/article/why-is-zoom-so-exhausting/

5. Rogelberg, S. G. Why meetings stink—and what to do about it. *Harvard Business Review.* https://hbr.org/2019/01/why-your-meetings-stink-and-what-to-do-about-it

6. Peters, J. (2020, April 28). Google's Meet teleconferencing service now adding about 3 million users per day. *The Verge.* https://www.theverge.com/2020/4/28/21240434/google-meet-three-million-users-per-day-pichai-earnings

7. Perlow, L. A., Hadley, C. N., & Eun, E. (2017, August). Stop the meeting madness. *Harvard Business Review.* https://hbr.org/2017/07/stop-the-meeting-madness

8. Time wasted in meetings: 21+ meeting statistics. (2023, October 2). *Bright Futures.* https://www.brightfuturesny.com/post/time-wasted-in-meetings

9. Goff-Dupont, S. (2022, February 24). How to run effective meetings in the era of hybrid work. *Atlassian.* https://www.atlassian.com/blog/teamwork/how-to-run-effective-meetings

10. Dewey, J. (1910). *How we think.* Heath.

11. O'Malley, M. (2019, December 12). What the "best companies to work for" do differently. *Harvard Business Review.* https://hbr.org/2019/12/what-the-best-companies-to-work-for-do-differently

12. Morse, R., & Brooks, E. (2023, September 17). How U.S. News calculated the 2024 best colleges rankings. *U.S. News & World Report.* https://www.usnews.com/education/best-colleges/articles/how-us-news-calculated-the-rankings

13. 2024 Niche college rankings. (2023). *Niche.* https://www.niche.com/colleges/rankings/

14. O'Malley (2019).

15. Rothwell, J. (2022). *In mixed company: Communicating in small groups and teams.* Oxford University Press.

16. Lublin, J. S. (2017, December 13). Talkaholics sink partnerships, presentations—and careers. *The Wall Street Journal.* https://www.wsj.com/articles/talkaholics-sink-partnerships-presentationsand-careers-1513173600

17. Yoerger, M., Allen, J. A., & Crowe, J. (2018). The impact of premeeting talk on group performance. *Small Group Research*, *49*, 226–258. https://journals.sagepub.com/doi/full/10.1177/1046496417744883

CHAPTER 16

1. Shonk, K. (2024, August 15). The trait theory of leadership. *Program on Negotiation, Harvard Law School.* https://www.pon.harvard.edu/daily/leadership-skills-daily/the-trait-theory-of-leadership/

2. Henricks, M. (2018, October 30). The mantle of leadership isn't held only by one pay grade. *Provoke Media.* https://www.holmesreport.com/latest/article/the-mantle-of-leadership-isn-t-held-only-by-one-pay-grade

3. Stewart, A. The myth of "born leaders." (2023, February 21). *Human Synergistics.* https://www.humansynergistics.com/en-ca/blog/2023/02/21/the-myth-of-born-leaders/

4. Shonk (2024).

5. Stogdill, R. M. (1948). Personal factors associated with leadership: A survey of the literature. *Journal of Psychology*, *25*, 35–71; Stogdill, R. M. (1974). *Handbook of leadership.* Free Press.

6. Buckingham, M., & Coffman, C. (1999). *First, break all the rules: What the world's greatest managers do differently.* Simon & Schuster.

7. Northouse, P. G. (2021). *Leadership: Theory and practice.* Sage.

8. Platow, M. J., Haslam, S. A., Reicher, S. D., & Steffens, N. K. (2015). There is no leadership if no-one follows: Why leadership is necessarily a group process. *International Coaching Psychology Review*, *10*, 20–37.

9. Moore, D. A., & Bazerman, M. H. (2022). *Decision leadership: Empowering others to make better choices.* Yale University Press.

10. Dutton, K. (2016, September–October). Would you vote for a psychopath? *Scientific American Mind*, *27*(5), 48–55.

11. Chamorro-Premuzic, T. (2019). *Why do so many incompetent men become leaders?* Harvard Business Review Press.

12. Drucker, P. F. (1988). The coming of the new organization. *Harvard Business Review*, *66*, 45–53.

13. Babiak, P., & Hare, R. D. (2006). *Snakes in suits: When psychopaths go to work.* HarperCollins.

14. Perman, C. (2011, September 2). Think your boss is a psychopath? That may be true. *CNBC.* http://www.cnbc.com//id/44376401

15. Croom, S. (2021, June 6). 12% of corporate leaders are psychopaths. *Fortune.* https://fortune.com/2021/06/06/corporate-psychopaths-business-leadership-csr/

16. Williams, R. (2015, January 27). The rise of toxic leadership and toxic workplaces. *Psychology Today*. https://www.psychologytoday.com/blog/wired -success/201601/the-rise-toxic-leadership-and-toxic-workplaces

17. Brunell, A. B., Gentry, W. A., Campbell, W. K., Hoffman, B. J., Kuhnert, K. W., & DeMarree, K. G. (2008). Leader emergence: The case of the narcissistic leader. Personality and *Social Psychology Bulletin*, *34*, 1663–1676. See also Nevicka, B., De Hoogh, A. H. B., & Hartog, D. N. D. (2018). Narcissistic leaders and their victims: Followers low on self-esteem and low on core self-evaluations suffer most. *Frontiers in Psychology*, *9*, 422. https://www.frontiersin.org/articles/10.3389/fpsyg.2018.00422/full #B40

18. Williams (2015).

19. Watts, A. L., Lilienfeld, S. O., Smith, S. F., Miller, J. D., Campbell, W. K., Waldman, I. D., Rubenzer, S. J., & Fashingbauer, T. J. (2013). The double-edge sword of grandiose narcissism: Implications for successful and unsuccessful leadership among U.S. presidents. *Psychological Science*, *24*, 2379–2389. https://doi.org/10.1177%2F0956797613491970

20. Nevicka, B., Ten Velden, F. S., De Hoogh, A. H. B., & Van Vianen, A. E. M. (2011). Reality at odds with perceptions: Narcissistic leaders and group performance. *Psychological Science*, *22*, 1259–1264.

21. Braun, S. (2017). Leader narcissism and outcomes in organizations: A review at multiple levels of analysis and implications for future research. *Frontiers of Psychology*. https://www.ncbi.nlm.nih.gov/pmc/articles /PMC5437163/

22. Chamorro-Premuzic (2019).

23. Hackman, M., & Johnson, C. (2019). *Leadership: A communication perspective*. Waveland Press.

24. Everest Leadership Academy. (2014, March). Critical leadership skills. *Ken Blanchard Companies*. http://www.everestla.org/images/pdfs/4_3 %20Critical%20Leadership%20Skills%20-%20Ken%20Blanchard.pdf

25. Goleman, D. (2013). *Focus: The hidden driver of excellence*. HarperCollins.

26. Erikson-Farr, B. (2023, October 5). What is your leadership style? *Gallup*. https://www.gallup.com/cliftonstrengths/en/511814/leadership-style .aspx

27. Rothwell, J. D., & Waters, M. (2023). *It's all of our business: Communicating competently in the workplace*. Oxford University Press.

28. Wu, Q., Cormican, K., & Chen, G. (2020). A meta-analysis of shared leadership: Antecedents,consequences, and moderators. *Journal of Leadership & Organizational Studies*, *27*, 49–64. https://journals.sagepub.com/doi/ full/10.1177/1548051818820862

CHAPTER 17

1. Zara, C. (2018, March 20). People were asked to name women tech leaders: They said "Alexa" and "Siri." *Fast Company*. https://www.fastcompany.com/40547212/people-were-asked-to-name-women-tech-leaders-they-said-alexa-and-siri

2. Hinchliffe, E. (2024, June 4). The share of Fortune 500 companies run by women CEOs stays flat at 10.4% as pace of change stalls. *Fortune*. https://fortune.com/2024/06/04/fortune-500-companies-women-ceos-2024/

3. Hinchliffe, E., & Abrams, J. (2023, August 2). Meet the 29 female CEOs who run a record-high 5.8% of the companies on Fortune's Global 500 list. *Fortune*. https://fortune.com/2023/08/02/fortune-global-500-female-ceos-women/

4. Women CEOs of the S&P 500 (list). (2023, February 3). *Catalyst*. https://www.catalyst.org/research/women-ceos-of-the-sp-500/

5. Leech, M. (2023, April 28). You are more likely to have a CEO named David than you are to have a woman at the helm, new report finds. *Bizwomen: The Business Journal*. https://www.bizjournals.com/bizwomen/news/latest-news/2023/04/you-are-more-likely-to-have-a-ceo-named-david-than.html

6. Women CEOs in underrepresented groups (list). (2022, March 29). *Catalyst*. https://www.catalyst.org/research/women-ceos-underrepresented-groups/

7. Boyle, M., & Green, J. (2023, April 25). Work shift: Women CEOs (finally) outnumber those named John. *Bloomberg*. https://www.bloomberg.com/news/newsletters/2023-04-25/women-ceos-at-big-companies-finally-outnumber-those-named-john

8. Nietzel, M. T. (2024, August 7). Women continue to outpace men in college enrollment and graduation. *Forbes*. https://www.forbes.com/sites/michaeltnietzel/2024/08/07/women-continue-to-outpace-men-in-college-enrollment-and-graduation/

9. Fry, R. (2022, September 26). Women now outnumber men in the U.S. college-educated labor force. *Pew Research Center*. https://www.pewresearch.org/short-reads/2022/09/26/women-now-outnumber-men-in-the-u-s-college-educated-labor-force/

10. Young, G. (2016, August 12). Women, naturally better leaders for the 21st century. *LeaderShape*. https://www.crcpress.com/rsc/downloads/WP-TL2-2016_Transpersonal_Leadership_WP2_FINAL.pdf

11. Kruse, K. (2023, March 31). New research: Women more effective than men in all leadership measures. *Forbes*. https://www.forbes.com/sites/kevinkruse/2023/03/31/new-research-women-more-effective-than-men-in-all-leadership-measures/

12. Novotney, A. (2023, March 23). Women leaders make work better. *American Psychological Association*. https://www.apa.org/topics/women-girls /female-leaders-make-work-better

13. Padavic, I., Ely, R. J., & Reid, E. M. (2019). Explaining the persistence of gender inequality: The work-family narrative as a social defense against the 24/7 work culture. *Administrative Science Quarterly*, 65, 61–111. https://doi .org/10.1177%2F0001839219832310

14. Ammerman, C., & Groysberg, B. (2021, May–June). How to close the gender gap. *Harvard Business Review*. https://hbr.org/2021/05/how-to-close -the-gender-gap

15. Silverman, R. W. (2015, September 30). Gender bias at work turns up in feedback. *The Wall Street Journal*. https://www.wsj.com/articles/gender -bias-at-work-turns-up-in-feedback-1443600759

16. Chira, S. (2017, June 14). The universal phenomenon of men inter-rupting women. *The New York Times*. https://www.nytimes.com/2017/06/14/ business/women-sexism-work-huffington-kamala-harris.html

17. Grant, A. (2021, February 18). Who won't shut up in meetings? Men say it's women. It's not. *The Washington Post*. https://www.washingtonpost .com/outlook/2021/02/18/men-interrupt-women-tokyo-olympics/

18. PON Staff. (2021, October 7). Three ways to ensure women in leader-ship are heard in group negotiations. *Program on Negotiation, Harvard Law School*. https://www.pon.harvard.edu/daily/negotiation-skills-daily/in-group -negotiations-make-sure-your-voice-is-heard-nb/

19. Peterson, S. J., Abramson, R., & Stutman, R. K. (2020, November–December). How to develop your leadership style. *Harvard Business Review*. https://hbr.org/2020/11/how-to-develop-your-leadership-style

CHAPTER 18

1. Noar, A. (2018, May 22). New survey results on presentations . . . #2 will shock you!*PresentationPanda*. https://presentationpanda.com/blog/new -presentation-statistics/

2. Gallo, C. (2021). Public speaking is no longer a "soft skill." It's your key to success in any field. *Inc*. https://www.inc.com/carmine-gallo/public -speaking-is-no-longer-a-soft-skill-its-your-key-to-success-in-any-field.html

3. Gallo, C. (2023, August 8). Build a winning mindset to unlock your public speaking potential. *Inc*. https://www.inc.com/carmine-gallo/build-a -winning-mindset-to-unlock-your-public-speaking-potential.html

4. The Chapman University survey on American fears. (2015, May 17). *Chapman University*. http://www.chapman.edu/wilkinson/_files/fear-2015/codebook.pdf

5. Marinho, A. C. F., Medeiros, A. M., Gama, A. C. C., & Teixeira, L. C. (2017). Fear of public speaking: Perception of college students and correlates. *Journal of Voice, 31*(1). https://doi.org/10.1016/j.jvoice.2015.12.012

6. Black, R. (2019, September 12). Glossophobia (fear of public speaking): Are you glossophobic? *Psycom*. https://www.psycom.net/glossophobia -fear-of-public-speaking

7. Kelakos, E. (2020, June 29). 5 ways to beat Zoom Performance Anxiety. *Eleni Group*. https://theelenigroup.com/2020/06/5-ways-to-beat-zoom -performance-anxiety-zpa/

8. The Chapman University survey on American fears (2015, May 17).

9. Bruskin-Goldring Report. (1993). America's number 1 fear—public speaking. Bruskin/Goldring; Thomson, J. (2008, October 24). A quarter of people fear public speaking more than dying—here's how to beat your fear. *Smartcompany.com*. https://www.smartcompany.com.au/technology/emerg-ing-technology/a-quarter-of-people-fear-public-speaking-more-than-dying -heres-how-to-beat-your-fear/

10. For detailed critiques, see Davies, J. W. (2011, September 25). Is there any real evidence that people are more afraid of public speaking than dying? *Quora.com*. http://www.quora.com/Is-there-any-real-evidence-that -people-are-more-afraid-of-public-speaking-than-dying; Tuttar, J. (2019). Is public speaking really more feared than death? *Speak and Conquer*. https:// speakandconquer.com/is-public-speaking-really-more-feared-than-death/

11. Star, K. (2018, June 10). 6 potential benefits of having anxiety: Positive effects that anxiety can create. *Verywellmind*. https://www.verywellmind.com /benefits-of-anxiety-2584134

12. Bodie, G. D. (2010). A racing heart, rattling knees, and ruminative thoughts: Defining, explaining, and treating public speaking anxiety. *Communication Education, 59*, 70–105. See also Tsaousides, T. (2017, November 27). Why are we scared of public speaking? *Psychology Today*. https://www .psychologytoday.com/us/blog/smashing-the-brainblocks/201711/why-are-we -scared-public-speaking

13. Dean, J. (2012, October 10). The illusion of transparency. *PsyBlog*. http://www.spring.org.uk/2012/10/the-illusion-of-transparency.php

14. MacInnis, C. C., MacKinnon, S. P., & MacIntyre, P. D. (2010). The illusion of transparency and normative beliefs about anxiety during public speaking. *Current Research in Social Psychology, 15*. http://www.uiowa.edu/ ~grpproc/crisp/crisp15_4.pdf

15. Savitsky, K., & Gilovich, T. (2003). The illusion of transparency and the alleviation of speech anxiety. *Journal of Experimental Social Psychology*, 39, 618–625.

16. Jackson, B., Compton, J., Thornton, A. L., & Dimmock, J. A. (2017). Re-thinking anxiety: Using inoculation messages to reduce and reinterpret public speaking fears. *PLOS ONE*. http://journals.plos.org/plosone/article?id=10.1371/journal.pone.0169972

17. Uncertainty reduction theory. (2019, January 9). *University of Twente*. https://www.utwente.nl/en/bms/communication-theories/sorted-by-cluster/Interpersonal-Communication-and-Relations/uncertainty-Reduction-theory/

18. Cuncic, A. (2021, June 25). The spotlight effect and social anxiety: Not everyone is staring at you. *Verywellmind*. https://www.verywellmind.com/what-is-the-spotlight-effect-3024470

19. Grieve, R., Woodley, J., Hunt, S. E., & McKay, A. (2021). Student fears of oral presentations and public speaking in higher education: A qualitative survey. *Journal of Further and Higher Education*. https://www.tandfonline.com/doi/full/10.1080/0309877X.2021.1948509. See also Jackson et al. (2017).

20. Witt, P. L., & Behnke, R. R. (2006). Anticipatory speech anxiety as a function of public speaking assignment type. *Communication Education*, 55, 167–177.

21. Swenson, A. (2011). You make my heart beat faster: A quantitative study of the relationship between instructor immediacy, classroom community, and public speaking anxiety. *UW-L Journal of Undergraduate Research*, 14, 1–12.

22. My colleague, Darrell Beck, devised this formula.

23. Tsaousides, T. (2017, November 28). How to conquer the fear of public speaking. *Psychology Today*. https://www.psychologytoday.com/us/blog/smashing-the-brainblocks/201711/how-conquer-the-fear-public-speaking

24. 24. Motley, M. T. (2011, January 18). Reducing public speaking anxiety: The communication orientation. *YouTube*. http://www.youtube.com/watch?v=GYfHQvi2NAg

CHAPTER 19

1. Sma, S., Schrift, R. Y., & Zauberman, G. (2018). The illusion of multitasking and its positive effect on performance. *Psychological Science*, 29, 1942–1955.

2. Wang, H.-T., Poerio, G., Murphy, D. B., Jefferies, E., & Smallwood, J. (2018). Dimensions of experience: Exploring the heterogeneity of the wandering mind. *Psychological Science, 29*, 56–71.

3. O'Keefe, D. (2016). *Persuasion: Theory and research.* Sage.

4. Quoted in Baram, M. (2009, June 8). Stephen Colbert Iraq show: Gen. Odierno shaves his head. *HuffPost.* http://www.huffingtonpost.com/2009/06/08/stephen-colbert-iraq-show_n_212388.html

5. Hogan, P. C. (2003). *The mind and its stories: Narrative universals and human emotion.* Cambridge University Press.

6. Hsu, J. (2008, August/September). The secrets of storytelling: Why we love a good yarn. *Scientific American Mind, 19*(4), 46–51. https://doi.org/10.1038/scientificamericanmind0808-46

7. Monarth, H. (2014, March 11). The irresistible power of storytelling as a strategic business tool. *Harvard Business Review.* https://hbr.org/2014/03/the-irresistible-power-of-storytelling-as-a-strategic-business-tool

8. Werk, N. (2017, December). The power of storytelling in research. *Quirk's Media.* https://www.quirks.com/articles/the-power-of-storytelling-in-research

9. Hershey, T. (2021). Living spiritual teachers project. *Spirituality & Practice.* https://www.spiritualityandpractice.com/explorations/teachers/terry-hershey/quotes

10. Friend, Z. (2013). *On message: How a compelling narrative will make your organization succeed.* Turner Publishing. See also Karia, A. (2015). *TED talks storytelling: 23 storytelling techniques from the best TED talks.* CreateSpace Independent Publishing Platform.

11. Friend (2013).

12. Quoted by McNiece, M. (2019, May 13). Ryan Reynolds: "Fatherhood is the best thing that ever happened to me." *People,* pp. 76–77.

13. Mehta, N. (2021, November 23). Laughing at different jokes: Humor across cultures. *Psychology Today.* https://www.psychologytoday.com/us/blog/non-weird-science/202111/laughing-different-jokes-humor-across-cultures

14. Dean, N. (2019, September 5). The importance of novelty. *Brain World Magazine.* https://brainworldmagazine.com/the-importance-of-novelty/

15. How to use ChatGPT to write a speech. (2023, March 15). AI-PRO. https://ai-pro.org/how-to-use-chatgpt-to-write-a-speech/

16. Iton, A. (2021). Root of COVID vaccine came from enslaved African American. *The Mercury News,* p. A6.

17. Ward-Glenton, H. (2022, November 8).Billionaires emit a million times more greenhouse gases than the average person: Oxfam. *CNBC.* https://www.cnbc.com/2022/11/08/billionaires-emit-a-million-times-more-greenhouse-gases-than-the-average-person-oxfam.html

18. Mirsky, S. (2017, April 3). Spiders gobble gargantuan numbers of tiny prey. *Scientific American*. https://www.scientificamerican.com/article/if-you-dont-like-insects-you-should-love-spiders/

CHAPTER 20

1. Miller, M. (2022, January). The myth of the moral open mind. *Manzanitamiller.com*. https://manzanitamiller.com/f/the-myth-of-the-moral-open-mind

2. Looking at "bothsidesing." (2024). *Merriam-Webster*. https://www.merriam-webster.com/wordplay/bothsidesing-bothsidesism-new-words-were-watching

3. Weingarten, G. (1994, September 27). I'm absolutely sure: You need a marshmallow enema. *San Jose Mercury News*, p.B7.

4. Kavanagh, J., & Rich, M. D. (2018). *Truth decay: An initial exploration of the diminishing role of facts and analysis in American public life*. RAND Corporation.

5. Vosoughi, S., Roy, D., & Aral, S. (2018).The spread of true and false news online. *Science*, 359,1146–1151.

6. Vallejo, J., & Thomas, P. (2022, January 18). Why some QAnon believers think JFK Jr is still alive—and about to become vice president. *Independent*. https://www.independent.co.uk/news/world/americas/us-politics/qanon-jfk-jr-alive-trump-b1995594.html

7. Hamilton, L. (2022, April 25). Conspiracy vs. science: A survey of U.S. public beliefs. *Carsey School of Public Policy*. https://carsey.unh.edu/publication/conspiracy-vs-science-survey-us-public-beliefs

8. Lawton, G. (2024). Conspiracy theories. *New Scientist*.

9. Enders, A., Farhart, C., Miller, J., Uscinski, J., Saunders, K., & Drochon, J. (2022, July 22). Are Republicans and conservatives more likely to believe conspiracy theories? *Political Behavior*. https://doi.org/10.1007/s11109-022-09812-3

10. Poppy, C. (2017, January/February). Survey shows Americans fear ghosts, the government, and each other. *Skeptical Inquirer*, pp. 16–18.

11. Berezow, A. (2016, January 26). Math's study shows conspiracies "prone to unravelling." *BBC News*. https://www.bbc.com/news/science-environment-35411684

12. Grossman, M. (2021, April 21). Conspiracy beliefs are not increasing nor exclusive to the right. *Niskanen Center*. https://www.niskanencenter.org/conspiracy-beliefs-are-not-increasing-or-exclusive-to-the-right/

13. Adler, J. E. (1998, January/February). Open minds and the argument from ignorance. *Skeptical Inquirer*, pp. 41–44.

14. Rothwell, J. D. (2023). *Practically speaking*. Oxford University Press.

15. Silver, N. (2012). *The signal and the noise: Why so many predictions fail—but some don't*. Penguin Press.

16. Quoted by Flam, F. (2021, February 26). Stop worrying about largely unlikely COVID-19 threats. *The Mercury News*, p. A6.

17. Sinatra, G., & Hofer, B. K. (2023, May 26). ChatGPT and other AI that fosters science denial. *Salon*. https://www.salon.com/2023/05/26/how -to-protect-yourself-from-chatgpt-and-other-ai-that-fosters-science-denial _partner/

18. Lauriello, S. (2022, December 2). How long does it take for the flu shot to be effective? *Health*. https://www.health.com/condition/flu/how-long -for-flu-shot-effective

19. Pinker, S. (2021). *Rationality: What it is, why it seems scarce, why it matters*. Viking.

20. Vigen, T. (2015). *Spurious correlations*. Hachette Books.

21. Sherman, E. (2009, March/April). Science and antiscience in America: Why it matters. *Skeptical Inquirer*, pp. 32–35; Silver (2012).

22. Silver (2012).

23. Sinusoid, D. (2022, February 2). Coincidence and the Law of Very Large Numbers. *Shortform*. https://www.shortform.com/blog/law-of-very -large-numbers/

24. Mathewson, S. (2016, August 10). How often do meteorites hit the Earth? *Space.com*. https://www.space.com/33695-thousands-meteorites- litter-earth-unpredictable-collisions.html

25. Nordquist, R. (2019, April 2). Hasty generalization (fallacy). *ThoughtCo*. https://www.thoughtco.com/hasty-generalization-fallacy-1690919

26. Schwartz, G. E. (2021). *Extraordinary claims require extraordinary evidence: The science and ethics of truth seeking and truth abuse*. Waterside Productions. See also Shermer, M. (2013, February 1). What is skepti- cism, anyway? *HuffPost*. https://www.huffpost.com/entry/what-is-skepticism- anyway_b_2581917

27. Shermer, M. (2016, September 1). Is it possible to measure super- natural or paranormal phenomena? *Scientific American*. https://www. scientificamerican.com/article/is-it-possible-to-measure-supernatural-or -paranormal-phenomena/

28. Pinker (2021).

29. Palmer, R. (2022, March/April). Twelve-year Australian skeptics study proves psychics fail . . . again and again and again. *Skeptical Inquirer*, p. 6.

30. Palminteri, S., Lefebvre, G., Kilford, E. J., & Blakemore, S.-J. (2017, August 11). Confirmation bias in human reinforcement learning: Evidence

from counterfactual feedback processing. *PLOS*. https://journals.plos.org/ploscompbiol/article?id=10.1371/journal.pcbi.1005684

CHAPTER 23

1. TV or not TV. (1993, April 19). *San Jose Mercury News*, p. 5E.

2. Blonde, J., & Girandola, F. (2016, March 14). Revealing the elusive effects of vividness: A meta-analysis of empirical evidences assessing the effect of vividness on persuasion. *Social Influence*. https://www.tandfonline.com/action/showCitFormats?doi=10.1080%2F15534510.2016.1157096

3. Ropeik, D. (2008, April 13). How risky is flying? *NOVA*. http://www.pbs.org/wgbh/nova/planecrash/risky.html

4. Westen, D. (2007). *The political brain: The role of emotion in deciding the fate of the nation*. PublicAffairs.

5. Novelly, T. (2018, June 3). Crowd cheers when valedictorian quotes Trump. Then reveals it was Obama. *USA Today*. https://www.usatoday.com/story/news/politics/2018/06/03/kentucky-valedictorian-quotes-trump-then-reveals-obama/667758002/Today

6. Yuan, Y., Sun, R., Zuo, J., & Chen, X. (2023, March). A new explanation for the attitude-behavior inconsistency based on the contextualized attitude. *Behavioral Sciences*. https://doi.org/10.3390/bs13030223

7. Gass, R., & Seiter, J. (2022). *Persuasion, social influence, and compliance gaining*. Allyn & Bacon.

8. Perloff, R. M. (2021). *The dynamics of persuasion: Communication and attitudes in the 21st century*. Routledge.

9. Gass and Seiter (2022).

10. Wallace, D. S., Paulson, R. M., Lord, C. G., & Bond, C. F. (2005). Which behaviors do attitudes predict? Meta-analyzing the effects of social pressure and perceived difficulty. *Review of General Psychology*, 9, 214–227.

11. Wallace et al. (2005, pp. 214–227).

12. Itkowitz, C. (2016, September 15). This Harvard professor explains why we were born to resist working out. *The Washington Post*. https://www.washingtonpost.com/news/inspired-life/wp/2016/09/15/this-harvard-professor-knows-why-you-skipped-the-gym-this-morning-it-is-natural-and-normal-to-be-physically-lazy/

13. Jordan, J. J., Sommers, R., Bloom, P., & Rand, D. G. (2017). Why do we hate hypocrites? Evidence for a theory of false signaling. *Psychological Science*, 28, 356–368.

14. Festinger, L. (1957). *A theory of cognitive dissonance*. Stanford University Press.

15. Quoted by Lord, L. (2021, January/February). Cognitive dissonance and the pandemic: A conversation with Carol Tavris. *Skeptical Inquirer*, pp. 57–61.

16. Pratkanis, A., & Aronson, E. (2001). *The age of propaganda: The everyday use and abuse of persuasion*. Freeman.

17. Lord (2021, pp. 57–61).

18. Tannenbaum, M., Wilson, K., Abarracin, D., Hepler, J., et al. (2015). Appealing to fear: A meta-analysis of fear appeal effectiveness and theories. *Psychological Bulletin, 141*, 1178–1204.

19. Montana Meth Project. (2022). About us. *MontanaMeth.org*. https://montanameth.org/about-us/#mission

20. Gass and Seiter (2022).

21. Tannenbaum et al. (2015, pp. 1178–1204).

22. Tannenbaum et al. (2015, pp. 1178–1204).

23. Tannenbaum et al. (2015, pp. 1178–1204).

24. Lennon, R., & Rentfro, R. (2010). Are young adults fear appeal effectiveness ratings explained by fear arousal, perceived threat and perceived efficacy? *Innovative Marketing, 6*, 58–65.

25. Rees, L., Friedman, R., Olekalns, M., & Lachowicz, M. (2020). Limiting fear and anger responses to anger expressions. *International Journal of Conflict Management*. https://www.emerald.com/insight/content/doi/10.1108/IJCMA-01-2019-0016/full/html

26. Turner, M. (2014, September 10). Anger appeals. In *Encyclopedia of health communication*. Sage. http://sk.sagepub.com/reference/encyclopedia-of-health-communication/n29.xml. See also Turner, M., Richards, A. S., Bessarabova, E., & Magid, Y. (2020). The effects of anger appeals on systematic processing and intentions: The moderating role of efficacy. *Communication Reports*. https://doi.org/10.1080/08934215.2019.1682175

27. Ilakkuvan, V., Turner, M. M., Cantrell, J., Hair, E., & Vallone, D. (2017). The relationship between advertising-induced anger and self-efficacy on persuasive outcomes: A test of the Anger Activism Model using the truth campaign. *Family and Community Health, 40*, 72–80.

28. Turner et al. (2020)

INDEX

ABOUT THE AUTHOR

J. Dan Rothwell is the former chair of the communication studies department at Cabrillo College. He was a communication studies professor at Western Washington University, Fort Hays Kansas State University, University of Oregon, and Lane Community College. He has a B.A. in American history from the University of Portland (Oregon), an M.A. in rhetoric and public address, and a Ph.D. in communication theory and social influence. His M.A. and Ph.D. are both from the University of Oregon. He is the author of six previous books. During his extensive career, he received more than two dozen teaching awards. His public speaking book, *Practically Speaking*, received the national "Textbook Excellence Award" from the Textbook and Academic Authors Association. Most recently, his coauthored book *It's All of Our Business* received the "Most Promising New Textbook Award" from the Textbook and Academic Authors Association.